Parenting

W9-ABT-063

$\frac{1}{23}$

FATHERS
AND SONS

ANTHOLOGIES EDITED BY DAVID SEYBOLD

Waters Swift and Still (with Craig Woods)
Seasons of the Hunter (with Robert Elman)
Seasons of the Angler
Boats
Fathers and Sons

FATHERS

An Anthology

AND SONS

Edited by David Seybold

Y GROVE WEIDENFELD

New York

Published by Grove Weidenfeld
A division of Grove Press, Inc.
841 Broadway
New York, NY 10003—4793

Published in Canada by General Publishing Company, Ltd.

Due to limitations of space, acknowledgments and permissions appear on page 197.

I would like to express my gratitude to Dan Green, who first suggested I compile and edit
this collection.—D.S.

Library of Congress Cataloging-in-Publication Data

Fathers and sons : an anthology / edited by David Seybold.—1st ed.
    p.   cm.
  ISBN 0-8021-1368-0 (acid-free paper)
  1. Fathers and sons—Literary collections.   2. American
literature—20th century.   I. Seybold, David.
PS509.F34F38   1992
810'.803520431—dc20   91-19945
                                                       CIP

Manufactured in the United States of America

Printed on acid-free paper

Designed by Irving Perkins Associates, Inc.

First Edition 1992

10 9 8 7 6 5 4 3 2 1

Illustration on title page by Dan Daly

For Mark and Alex Polizzotti—father and son

CONTENTS

FOREWORD

Somewhere in my family's midden of photographic slides is a close-up shot, taken by my wife, of our two-year-old son flying. He is burly and blond in the photo, laughing, stubby arms and legs spread, surrounded by nothing at all except blue sky. I have thrown him a couple of feet above my head into the air, though the picture does not show this. My hands, out of sight below the frame of the photo, are stretched upward—still are, in another, broader-framed shot taken a moment later—and when time unfreezes I will catch him again. Until then he is safe, and I am strong and confident.

More photos, twenty-four years newer: In the first, my son, grinning like a fool, holds his week-old baby boy in one hand. Not cradled with one arm, as a baby or a sack of groceries usually is held, but cupped in his hand, as if the baby were a softball or a grapefruit. My grandson, born three weeks early, is so small, and my son, who is nearly six feet five inches tall, is so big, that the hand overlaps the child. Another shot, six months later: The baby is burly and strong. He laughs as his happy young father, sure enough, tosses him a couple of inches into the air.

I do not throw my grandson into the air, though I could do it easily. I hold him and play with him, but grandfather does not toss grandson. That sort of perilous, crazy love is not in the franchise.

What strikes me about the stories collected here, under the

franchise of fathers and sons, is their desperate intensity, and their quality of melancholy. Mothers and daughters can spill it out, usually; hope and bitterness, resentment, reproach, love. Men can't, and are haunted. I don't think the sad and wistful fad that has males drumming in the woods these days will help much.

Years ago I visited my parents after being away for several months, and realized with a flare of anger, twisted with fear, that my father was old. "Lay off!" I wanted to tell him, absurdly, though I was past thirty myself. "Just cut it out; I don't want you old." But I swallowed my feelings, and half a year later when he retired from medicine, I wrote him a letter saying that I was proud of him. It was the best I could do.

Most of the sons and the fathers who write here have felt something like that, I'd guess. One result is that there is very little in editor David Seybold's *Fathers and Sons* that is light or jokey, very little that is tricked-up and literary. What you have are men trying hard, at last, to talk about important matters, about love and shame and self-loaded expectations too heavy to carry. One sentence from Jim Fergus's "My Father's Son" sets the echoes ringing: "I am just the age now that my father was when I was born." Another of those talisman sentences, the beginning of Ken Barrett's "Promises," reads: "When my father died we were both too young." Yes, always.

Intensity and loss and high emotion don't guarantee clear passage through a job of writing, but an impressive number of the writers here, it seems to me, have fought their demons and gotten things right. Read Kent Nelson's "The Middle of Nowhere." Read Wesley McNair's brief and stinging poem, a distilled novel really, called "After My Stepfather's Death." Read Sydney Lea's "The Buzzards." And read, especially, Charles Gaines's "Cooking the Rat," the best and truest pages this very good novelist and essayist has done.

The phone rings. My son, jobless and split now from his own son's mother, is looking for work in Colorado. He asks about the baby, then is silent. You there? Yeah. Then he says he has found an apartment, and thinks he may have a ski patrolling job. Could I . . . ?

Sure, I say, how much do you need? He tells me. No, it's okay, I say; I can handle that. No, it's not a problem. Take care, hope it all works out. Keep in touch.

We hang up, having said nothing, two men who love each other. Best we could do.

—John Skow

"He felt that although his father loved their home and loved all of them, he was more lonely than the contentment of this family love could help; that it even increased his loneliness, or made it hard for him not to be lonely. He felt that sitting out here, he was not lonely; or if he was, that he felt on good terms with the loneliness; that he was a homesick man, and that here on the rock, though he might be more homesick than ever, he was well. He knew that a very important part of his well-being came of staying a few minutes away from home, very quietly, in the dark, listening to the leaves if they moved, and looking at the stars; and that his own, Rufus' own presence, was fully as indispensable to this well-being. He knew that each of them knew of the other's well-being, and of the reason for it, and knew how each depended on the other, how each meant more to the other, in this most important of all ways, than anyone or anything else in the world."

—JAMES AGEE, *A Death in the Family*

"There is no good father, that's the rule."

—JEAN-PAUL SARTRE, *The Words*

FATHERS
AND SONS

COOKING THE RAT

by Charles Gaines

In *Iron John*, Robert Bly's book on men and manhood, Bly quotes an African story about hunting, food, and fatherhood. One day, a father takes his son hunting with him. The father kills a small rat and gives it to the son to keep, but the son, thinking it nothing, tosses it into the bush. They find no more game that day, and at dusk the father asks the boy for the rat so he can cook it for their supper. "I threw it in the bush," says the boy. Then, goes the story, "The father took up his axe, and hit his son, who was knocked unconscious; and the father then left the boy lying where he was."

When I first read that story, I could see the axe falling. I could see it hit the boy where his neck meets his shoulder, and the boy was me. Says Bly, "Men who hear [this] story know in the most astonishing detail exactly where that axe blow fell. One says the axe hit the left side of his head. Another said it landed in the chest area. Another said 'On my shoulder' . . . and so on and so on. Almost every man remembers that blow coming in. So this event seems to be a part of father-son material: the father gives a blow and the son gets it. And it's a wound the boy remembers for years."

If only we had not thrown away the rat! Instead of lying unconscious in an oblivion of shame, we would have feasted with our fathers on small haunches and celebrated the hunt, with no wound

4   CHARLES GAINES

to be remembered for years. But we did, most of us. Most of us threw away the rat.

Here is another story about hunting, food, and fatherhood.

It is the 1950s in Birmingham, Alabama. The father in this story lives in a big house that he bought with money he made from working very hard for his wife's family, though he never much liked to work. Working hard for his wife's family and not liking it, along with drinking too much red whiskey, has given him an ulcer, a self-inflicted wound that will almost kill him. He is a big, charming man who has never met a stranger, popular in board rooms, in private clubs, and on shooting plantations. He is a civic leader, a great dancer, someone who will fight with his fists and relish it, a devoted husband, a lover of sensation and travel but not of mystery, a bigot, a sentimental realist with precise hands and head, immutable values, a sense of humor, no fear of death, a fine, sartorial flair, and no religion beyond hunting and fishing. He knows exactly what he likes and doesn't like, what he believes and doesn't believe. He has absolutely no pretense, and, though he is an honors graduate of M.I.T., not the slightest intellectual inclination or urge to ponder his life. He is virile yet high-strung—a saber blade ornately scrolled. And he is a clear sky with one low, dark cloud in it.

Within ten years he will quit drinking overnight and never touch another drop, but for now he is a fierce and secret drunk. He hides quart bottles of bourbon from his wife in laundry hampers, his gun closet, the kitchen pantry. And when she is gone, he swoops down on them like a hawk on chickens. He makes an effort to hide his drinking, and himself when he is drunk, from his wife and his daughter. But not from his son.

Every autumn the father takes his family on a trip to New York City, where they stay in a grand hotel and go to musicals and toy stores and eat in French restaurants. Some nights, after the mother and daughter have gone to bed, the father takes the son out for a walk. When they leave the hotel, the son can still smell the perfume of the women at dinner, and he hears "Marie," a song that for some reason means New York to him, playing in his head. The uptown streets are bright and soul stirring. They stop in a bar or two, never for long. The son studies exhilarated Yankee faces and believes they know some secret he will never learn in Birmingham. He sings to himself, "Marie, the dawn is breaking . . ."

Usually, the father and son end up at Luchows, a German restaurant the father likes. The son eats chocolate ice cream while waiters in black aprons bring the father mug after mug of German beer. If anyone annoys the father on the way back to the hotel, he will probably offer to fight them. Once a man on Park Avenue accepted and the son watched his father hit this man in the face so that his hat flew off. Except for when he is picking fights, the father is usually in a jolly mood on these late-night trips abroad on the New York streets, and so is the son. Wrapped in a Brooks Brothers overcoat, he sits next to his big, drunk, well-dressed father in the back of a warm taxi going back uptown to their suite overlooking Central Park, and he knows that life is an oyster you need the right tool and technique to open. "Marie, you'll soon be waaking . . ." he sings to himself in the back of the cab, and the song wraps around him like a silver belt.

At the time of this story, the son is twelve years old, on the verge of a disastrous adolescence. He will be thrown out of private schools for reasons ranging from arrogance to laziness to venereal disease. Between these schools, he will float over the country as if it were a bazaar, picking through a booth here, a booth there, for experiences. He is vain, feckless, and light, with a grandiose sense of himself that buoys and floats him over his own life. It will be years before he knows anything worth knowing. Even at twelve, he is a trial for the father, but not yet the desperate misery he will become. This son was born believing he could decide whether or not a rat is big enough to keep, and the wounds he receives for his wrong judgments will soon put him into a trance. For years, he will live in that trance, and when he finally wakes as a grown man, he will remember very little of what really happened to him in all those years.

So: It is a November afternoon and the father and son are alone in the big house in Alabama. The mother and sister are out of town and it is the cook's and maids' day off. The father is just home from work, still dressed in his suit—striped tie pulled away from his throat—and he is drinking. He is standing in the kitchen drinking bourbon whiskey straight from a bottle that was hidden in the pantry and the son is there with him.

The son hopes the father will talk to him. What he really hopes is that the suit of armor that is his father will teeter once or twice, creak, and fall over; that it will lie on the kitchen floor and that birds will finally fly out from its open visor and fill the house. But a conversation will do.

"We're going hunting. Go get your pellet rifle," says the father.

He seems happy, and the son feels a dark, thrilling flutter in his stomach.

"*Hunting*? You mean at Midway? Now?"

Midway, where they go to hunt quail, is a three-hour drive away.

"Not at Midway." The father puts the bottle into a drawer and closes it. "Just come on. Go get your gun."

They take the son's pellet rifle and a shotgun into the backyard. It is a big backyard, with well-spaced oak and hickory and pine trees. It is a warm evening, almost dusk. The father, still wearing his business shirt and tie, carries the side-by-side shotgun into the yard, and the son follows, pumping up his pellet rifle. He watches his father's white shirt move through the darkening air, weaving a little against the black trees, and he tries hard to breathe evenly. He has had the pellet rifle for a year and he has shot a few songbirds and a squirrel or two with it. For two seasons at Midway he has shot a pellet pistol, futilely, at covey rises of quail, and his father has told him that when he kills a quail in that way he will be allowed to shoot a shotgun. Within a year, the son will kill a quail with the pistol and earn the same Winchester shotgun the father is now carrying, and after many more years he will finally learn how to hunt. Now he only wants to know how to kill with purpose, and he can hardly breathe from the suddenness and strangeness of this lesson and from the realization that he wanted it.

The black trees are full of squirrels. Mourning doves, fed and encouraged throughout the neighborhood, clatter in the branches.

"There's a squirrel," says the father, pointing into a hickory tree. "Kill it."

The son can see the squirrel's back humped along a branch. He trembles as he pulls the trigger and misses. The father laughs. The squirrel runs around the tree and they follow it. It is lower now, hugging the trunk and the son kills it. The father shoots the head off a mourning dove and when a second one flies out of the tree, he drops it with the second barrel. The Winchester booms insult to the neighborhood, reverberating among the big houses. The father is laughing, laughing. He squeezes the back of the boy's neck with his big hand, and the son can feel in the strength and gaiety of his hand his lifelong unconcern for consequences. They kill another squirrel and two more doves, and then, in the dark, they go back inside the house to the big, bright kitchen.

The father takes the bottle from the drawer again and drinks thirstily from it. He is all energy and intent now. He pulls out roasting pans, skillets, garlic, bacon. The son has never seen either of his parents cook. In this house meals are cooked behind closed doors, then served in a dining room, by people paid to do those things. He watches the father's banging, spilling, joyful preparations to build a meal for the two of them and is hit by a heat coming off of it, as if the father had made a fire in the middle of the room.

They clean the game together at the kitchen table, plucking and drawing the doves, skinning and quartering the squirrels. Pearl gray dove feathers hang in the air. Their hands are bloody. The trash can is full of small entrails. Feather and fur spill onto the table and floor. Flushed and animated, the father talks and talks about shooting and cooking, fishing and cooking: about using ginger root with fried bass, duck curry, pompano in a brown bag. He is talking as he wraps the doves in bacon and shoves them in the oven, as he rubs the squirrels with garlic, dips them in egg and corn meal, and drops them into two cast-iron skillets full of smoking oil, as he pours the last of the whiskey into a water glass, half filling it, to drink with his meal. They eat at the kitchen table off of plastic servants' plates. They pull the meat off the bones with their fingers and leave the carcasses on the table, let them fall to the floor. They eat fiercely, as if they were hungry for more than food—as if it were only one rat they shared and they were a long way from home, huddled over a small fire after a long day of danger and adventure. And when the father and the son leave the kitchen, they leave it with no dish or pan washed, no spilled blood or dropped bone cleaned up; they just walk away, as if leaving an old campsite.

Later that night, the son is upstairs in bed. It is late and the room is dark, but the son is not yet asleep. He realizes that he has been waiting for an answer from his father for a long time and that he has finally been given that answer. His father, he realizes, has told him what he can and cannot have from the father. The son is trying to puzzle out the answer, to get it right, but he can't. And he never does. Years later, after he has many times served himself up to his own sons, he has an image of his father that night, serving himself on the platter of his manhood to the boy in the kitchen. It is a fine, sturdy, handsome old platter with repaired cracks running through it, and it is chipped at the edges, but it never leaks.

Now the father comes into the son's dark bedroom through the bathroom they share and sits on the bed. He is backlit by the open bathroom door and the son cannot see the expression on his face. He sees the big shoulders, the uncombed hair, and he smells whiskey. The father bends and hugs the son to him, holding him lightly. Over the next few years, through the seasickness and fear and hurricane winds of the son's adolescence, the father will do this often, late at night after he has had to whip the son; he will come in late, smelling hard of whiskey and hug the son to him, and the hug will feel to the son at those times like iron, like the cold at sea, like the embrace of hopelessness. Now the hug is just a nod and a smile at the quiet end of conversation over a fire.

THE MIDDLE OF NOWHERE

by Kent Nelson

I

This happened just after I'd dropped out of high school, when I was seventeen and living with my father. We had this trailer out southwest of Tucson, about twenty-three miles, right at the edge of the Papago Reservation, at the end of a dirt road which petered out into the Baboquivari Mountains. Across to the east you could see the Sierritas, which were a low rim of jagged hills, and to the south there was not much of anything except saguaros and greasewood and mesquite and the highway which ran from Robles Junction to Sasabe on the Mexican border.

Our trailer sat on a hill above two sand gullies. The previous occupants had seen fit to throw their trash into the steeper ravine, but the other one was a nice broad wash, rocky in places, with good cover for deer in the thickets of paloverde and ironwood. There were a couple of other trailers back down toward the highway, their TV antennas and satellite dishes the main evidence that someone else lived out there. Now and then you could hear a dog barking at the coyotes at night.

By this time in my life I'd pretty much seen everything. I don't mean I had anything figured cold or that I possessed some ultimate

9

knowledge—pretty much the opposite was true. I mean, nothing surprised me anymore. When I was nine and ten I lived with my mother in Phoenix, and she had done about everything I could imagine. She drank and went on benders, leaving me in the apartment for two or three days at a time. And it was a crummy building. People got beaten up there, and one man got killed. I watched him get carried out on a stretcher.

My mother had boyfriends, too. When a man stayed over, I slept on the sofa instead of in the one bed my mother and I shared. Through the thin walls I could hear my mother calling out a stranger's name. When the man liked me, it was all right; but when he didn't, which was more usual, I got shipped down on the Greyhound to my father.

I didn't mind it in Tucson. My father had a house in the barrio then, and there were lots of people moving around the streets at all hours. I liked to watch them doing their deals and loving up and just walking around. I liked the sirens and the shouts in Spanish and the music.

Sometimes I stayed a few days, sometimes a few weeks. But always a time came to go back.

"You sure you want to go?" my father used to ask.

"Why wouldn't I?"

"Your mother's not very well," he said. "She's fragile."

"I can take care of her."

The truth was, I didn't know whether I wanted to go back. I didn't much like the apartment on the eighth floor or my mother's boyfriends. My father's girlfriends were nicer. But I kept thinking of my mother's sad face and how much she wanted to be happy.

So it went that way for a long time, back and forth between Phoenix and Tucson. I tried to get my mother to take better care of herself—to go to sleep earlier so she could get to her job, which was in a plant nursery over in Mesa, to eat better, and not to drink so much. She did all right for a while, until she met this man named Ray, who started her on some pills. Then Ray moved in and I went off to Tucson, thinking I'd stay for good.

My father and I got along pretty well. He was a spindly man, wiry, very good-looking in a rough way. He had good hands and a sleek brown mustache, and he was a smooth talker. I was softer like my mother, and more inclined to observation. We weren't close in the sense of camaraderie or talking things out. We didn't discuss things much, so there were spaces around us unfilled, like something left unsaid late at night. Maybe he felt guilty about leaving.

I spent a whole school year with my father when I was sixteen, and saw my mother only once. That was the fall she got sick and went to the hospital, and she called for me. I guess I knew she was dying because I asked her questions I never had thought of before—what she used to be like when she was a girl in California, about her parents I'd never met (they owned a small artichoke farm), what she had hoped for in life. She couldn't speak very well. By then she was sleeping most of the time, and she'd wake up only for brief glimpses of me. She'd start describing a place she remembered or a special day, then suddenly drift off into a terrible stillness.

When she died, I was left hanging.

After that I decided not to go back to school. I hadn't been a bad student or a troublemaker; I just hadn't done anything. I wrote my homework but couldn't turn it in, and even when I knew an answer in class, I'd sit with my head down on the desk. The teachers talked to me; they sent me to counselors. Why wouldn't I try? Why not cooperate? They even got my one friend, George White Foot, a half-breed Apache, to speak to me. But finally they gave up and let me seep down into groundwater.

About this time was when my father got hold of the trailer. He had been evicted from his house, which was going to be torn down to make way for some renewal project, but I suspected he had other reasons for wanting to be out of town. He liked women. He had a way with them, too, but unlike my mother, he wanted the relationships to be simple. My mother was in love with every man she met. She'd say, "Stevie, he's so wonderful. What do you think?"

But my father liked things uncomplicated, and one way to keep them that way was to live out in a trailer in the middle of nowhere.

So I stayed out at the trailer for the next year. My father might have made me get a job, but in a way I had the upper hand. My mother had left me a few thousand dollars, and I was able to pay my share of rent and food. Now and then I'd go into Tucson to the library or a movie, but mostly I stayed home, as if I were waiting for something to happen; I didn't know what. It wasn't exactly waiting; it was passing time. It was as if everything up to then had been a test of endurance, and I had to recover from it. I needed to rest.

I spent some time watching the cars float along the highway in the distance, imagining who was in them and what future they were headed toward. I could see pickup trucks coming from Mexico, red sedans, half-tons, vans. At night the headlights skimmed through the darkness like comets.

For a month I exhumed the trash in the ravine and tried to piece together the lives of the people who'd lived there before. I couldn't come up with much except that they were poor and someone had done a good trade with whoever sold Jim Beam.

But mostly I took target practice with the .22, and I read. I read everything I could get my hands on. My father brought me books and magazines whenever he happened to think of me—from the 7-Eleven, from someone's house where he was repairing an air conditioner or a washing machine, from a friend's apartment, sometimes even from the bookmobile parked in the mall where his appliance repair company had its dispatch office. He never asked me what I liked. His idea was that in the general variety he'd hit on something that would move me off high-center. He gave me manuals about engines, a history of Vietnam, a book on oil painting, porno magazines, English novels. I imagined him standing in front of a library shelf or a magazine rack wondering what to choose. What should he take home to a son about whom he had not the slightest notion?

But I knew him. His whole life was women. He met women in bars or on the job or at diners, supermarkets, offices, even at the bookmobile. He had a gift for it, a genius. Educated or uneducated; black, white, Hispanic; tall or short: He could have charmed the underwear off a nun.

He had a system worked out. He'd bring a woman for a night and take her back to Tucson in the morning. It'd be dark when they'd get there—a turn at Robles Junction, head west on gravel, keep left when the road forked, and so on. The woman would be riding blindfolded, so to speak. There was no telephone, so she could never call.

Sometimes he'd bring someone home on a Friday night, and she'd stay until Monday. I dreaded these weekends because my father worked half days on Saturdays, and often overtime, and he'd leave the woman, whoever she was, with me. On such occasions the woman usually slept late. Once, one slept all day without stirring, and I was certain she was dead; and another one, when she woke up late and looked out the window, thought she'd been sent to hell.

But the worst thing was there were no introductions. Sometimes my father hadn't even told the woman I was there, and more than once a woman I'd never seen before came naked from my father's bedroom and, seeing me, started screaming. After a few times, I made it a habit on Saturday mornings to take target practice with the .22 from the kitchen window.

Even that wasn't enough every time. Once, despite a half hour's fusillade from the porch on a dead washing machine, a blonde came out half naked. She was twenty-four or so, hung over, but still pretty, even with her makeup smudged. All she had on were a pair of green panties and a blouse with one button fastened.

"Who is it?" she asked, shielding her eyes from the sun and peering off into the gully.

"Indians."

She moved to the rail of the landing. "Where?"

"You'd better go back inside," I told her. "We're the only wagon train in this circle."

She nodded. "You come with me," she said. She walked by and dragged her fingers across my shoulder. "I'd feel safer."

But I didn't go. I spent the rest of the morning at the edge of the yard shooting the arms off saguaros.

That wasn't the only incident like that either. I had the idea my father asked some of his lesser friends to flirt with me, but it was a suspicion I never proved.

One rainy afternoon when he was late, for example, I was reading in the living room, listening occasionally to the barrage on the tin roof. Out the window, little waterfalls collected from nowhere and rushed into the gullies. The sandwash was a torrent. Then this woman, whose name was Jake, came to the window. Maybe she was watching for my father; maybe she thought he'd never get there in the storm. Maybe she was bored. Anyway, she turned to me and said, "Steve, do you want to make love?"

"Who-what?"

"Don't you think I'm pretty?"

Jake was pretty. She had a smooth oval face and dark eyes, and nice high breasts which stood out under my father's shirt. "I think you're very pretty."

"Well then?"

"You're my father's girl."

She made a face that was supposed to show hurt or maybe defiance, but which made her look spoiled. "I'm not anybody's girl," she said.

I won't say I wasn't tempted. Under ordinary circumstances I wouldn't have cared whose girl she was, but these were not ordinary circumstances. I wanted to kiss her and slap her both. I wanted to shake her. What did she mean offering herself like that? But I didn't say anything.

She came over and put her hand on my arm, and I felt a terrible dark chill run through me like a sliver of cold steel. In that instant I knew what torture my mother must have suffered to be so helpless in desire. But the rain stopped abruptly. The drumming on the roof ebbed to a hum, and not far down the gravel road, the headlights of my father's truck delved through the steam rising from the hot earth.

There was one woman who stayed nearly a month. Her name was Esther, and she'd just been divorced from a doctor in Tucson and was waiting to hear about a nursing job in Los Angeles. She didn't have a place to stay, so my father said "What the hell," and she came to the trailer.

She was not so pretty as most of the women my father had. She had curly hair and a broad face and rather sad blue eyes which looked right at you, which I liked. We used to drink beer together in the afternoons and play gin rummy at the kitchen table. She never asked about my father like some women did. Instead she asked about my mother: What was she like, what did she do, where was she? Why did she and my father get divorced?

I was usually a little drunk, and trying to answer was like exploring a region of myself I'd never encountered. I went down one wrong path after another, found dead ends, labyrinths. If I forced words too quickly, I missed details; if I labored too long, I became lost in a confusion of images. At the same time, I understood it was important to try. No matter what fleeting impression I gave, no matter how mystified I felt, I needed to know who my mother was to know who I was.

Esther didn't hurry me. She'd listen one day and the next. She'd fetch new beers. She was as solid as I was shaky. Her own divorce, she said, made her tougher, and she knew what she wanted. I admired her patience, and I remember it seemed hopeful to me at the time that someone could choose to change her life, get on a bus one day, and do it.

After Esther left for L.A. there was a month or so when my father didn't bring anyone home. During this stretch, George White Foot showed up one day with a bottle of tequila, which we took down into the sandwash, along with the .22. George said he'd run into my father in a bar, and my father said I was anxious for company.

George had quit school, too. He was bagging groceries temporarily at the Safeway and thinking of going over to Safford to work in the copper mine. "You want to go?" he asked. "I got Apaches who can get you in." He gulped the tequila.

"I'm not done here yet," I said.

George nodded. "What are you doing out here?"

"Taking notes."

He laughed and drank some more. "Taking notes on what?"

I didn't have an answer. I thought I was taking notes. I sighted the rifle and picked off a cholla blossom. "I bet I can outshoot you," I said. "I'll stand, and you can shoot prone. A dollar a target."

"You have to drink some tequila," he said.

I drank some tequila, and George picked the targets, and I beat him five times in a row.

"Where'd you get the name White Foot?" I asked.

"Where'd you get the name Steve?"

He sat down in the sand and skewered the bottle down and took off his tennis shoes and socks. One of his feet was brown like his arms, but the other was albinistic—almost totally white up to the ankle.

I took off my boots and my socks. "I got two of them."

We laughed and drank more tequila, and he called me Steve White Feet. "I'll bet the five dollars I owe you you can't give me the right question to the answer 'sis-boom-bah.' "

I pretended to think for a minute, but nothing came to mind. "I don't know."

"Guess."

I didn't want to guess. I was getting drunk and it struck me that George couldn't go to work in the copper mine in Safford, even though that was where the Apaches had their land. "Don't go, George," I said.

He stared at me. He was drunker than I was. "Don't you want to know the question?" he asked.

"I want to know every question."

"An exploding sheep."

He laughed, but it wasn't funny.

We finished the bottle of tequila, and after that we staggered up the sandwash to hunt rabbits. But by then the rabbits were safe.

II

It was late fall when something changed. The long-day heat was out of the rocks, and I had found a ledge behind an outcropping where I could sit and read and see nothing at all except the blue Sierritas and farther away the Las Guijas hills and the Santa Ritas. Now and then through my binoculars I'd watch a hawk drifting on the updrafts which poured from the ravines.

Then one evening my father came home early with a stack of books from the bookmobile and some groceries. He actually sat down in the living room.

"I'm going to stay in town for a couple of days," he said.

"Oh yeah? What's her name?"

"Don't be that way."

"What way? I just asked what her name was."

"Goldie."

I didn't think much of it at the time. My father didn't often stay in town, but that was his business, and it didn't matter to me one way or the other. He didn't give me the details, and I didn't ask.

"You be okay?"

"Sure," I said. "Thanks for the books."

A couple of days later I was on the ledge, and I heard the horn of my father's truck. I scrambled up to the ridge where I could see down to the trailer. In the circle of my binoculars, I made out my father standing on the porch beside a short-haired, dark-haired woman. He was waving for me to come down.

I figured this was Goldie, though I'd imagined her as a blonde. She looked tall from a distance, as tall as my father anyway, who was six feet. She wore fancy sandals, and he had on cowboy boots. She looked like some kind of real estate person, dressed in a gray business suit, or maybe a social worker, and for a moment I wondered whether my father had some deal going, some scam. Then a piece of sunlight flashed from one of her earrings.

When I had climbed down into the sandwash and halfway up the hill, they appeared at the lip of the trail above me. I paused amidst the tangle of cholla and ocotillo and looked up. The woman's hair, which I'd thought was short, was pushed up on top of her head in a twist. The gray business suit was a sweater and slacks. I guessed she was about thirty, maybe a little older.

What impressed me most, though, was not the way she looked; it was the way my father looked. He kept motioning for me to hurry, and he had a grin on his face that seemed to say he had this secret he couldn't wait to tell me. He must have won the lottery, I thought, the way he was grinning.

"Steve," he said. "Come on up here. This is Goldie. Goldie, this is my boy, Steve."

I climbed the last few yards, and Goldie took a step forward and put out her hand.

I took her hand, felt her smooth palm. "You don't look like a Goldie," I said.

She squeezed my hand and smiled. "You don't look like a boy."

When I heard her voice, I knew she was not the lottery representative or a real estate lady or like any of the other women who'd ever been to the trailer before. Her voice slid over words with a lilting inflection like water over slick rock, or maybe like the chinooks blow under the eaves of the tin roof.

"She's Irish," my father said. "I met her on a job at her uncle's place out Gates Pass. We've been up at the Grand Canyon for a couple of days."

"Your father rescued me," Goldie said. She gave a small, sweet laugh.

"I thought, if she wants, she might as well stay out here awhile," my father said. "What do you think, Steve?"

He'd never asked me before what I thought. "Sounds all right to me," I said. "If she wants."

Right away it was strained. Goldie liked privacy, and in a trailer privacy's as scarce a commodity as snow in hell. From back to front there was a bedroom, a hallway up one wall which joined the bathroom, and a second, smaller bedroom where I slept. The kitchen opened into the living room. Whenever Goldie wanted to use the bathroom, she knocked to make certain it was empty. And when she walked around the house, she had on at least a robe. In some ways it would have been easier having around a woman who didn't mind being seen half undressed, even a flaunter, than one who was so prissy about things.

She also changed the hours of our days. My father didn't go drink in bars anymore, which was his usual habit. Even when Esther was here for that month, he might as well have been in a bar because as soon as he got home he took her to bed. But with Goldie it was more civilized. When my father got home and tried to talk her into going to bed, she'd laugh and say in a voice both teasing and gentle, "You're nothing but a rotten Englishman."

Goldie wanted to learn to cook—not necessarily fancy things, but something more substantial than hamburgers. She was anxious to try rabbit and venison and rattlesnake, and she liked Mexican food— burritos, jalapeño omelettes, enchiladas—which my father and I were pretty good at. So the three of us ate dinners at a normal hour. She called me Stephen, and I called her Blackie, and we talked about whatever happened to strike Goldie's fancy.

I could take the knocking on the bathroom door and the robe and the family dinners, but I chafed under Goldie's idea that the day started at five A.M. I liked to stay up late and read and then sleep in the next morning. To hear Goldie making coffee in the dark drove me crazy. The kettle whistled, and she clanked silverware, and unscrewed the jar of instant and got out the milk. Then the front door opened and closed. I'd lie there as gray light seeped through the window, angry, unable to sleep. What was she doing outside? And how long was my father going to let this last?

Once I got up to see where she went at that hour. I expected to see her down the road, taking a walk, or maybe doing calisthenics in the yard, or praying—something like that. But when I opened the door, she was sitting on the porch steps bundled up in a wool coat against the chill of the desert. Her coffee was steaming into the air.

"What the hell are you doing?" I asked.

"Sometimes I miss Ireland," was all she said.

For those first several weeks, she went into town with my father in the mornings. She borrowed his truck and toured the countryside— the Desert Museum, the mission of San Xavier, the university, the Pima Air Museum. She ranged as far as Phoenix and Nogales, and even drove by herself through the Papago Reservation to Puerto Peñasco on the Gulf of California.

She asked me to go with her once. It was on one of those stormy days when low-flying clouds banked into the Baboquivaris and slipped over into the basin. I couldn't go up to my ledge, so I said all right, I'd go. She wanted to go into the Catalinas—to the top of

Mount Lemmon. So that's what we did. The road started in ocotillo and saguaro along Tanque Verde Drive and wound up into oaks and sycamores. A warm misty rain was falling. But when we got higher into the pines it was snowing. I'd seen snow before but had been in it only once, up in Flagstaff when I was about nine. My mother had gone up to surprise a man—just the scene my father hated. This man said he owned a sporting goods store, and we went to every store in Flagstaff before we found him. It turned out he was a salesman, and he obviously wasn't expecting to see my mother. She sent me outside to play, and it was snowing on the streets. I remember how dirty the snow seemed, mashed down by tires and turning the buildings gray.

But at the top of Mount Lemmon the snow was clean. The pale trees were ghostly as the air, and even the road was white and unmarked.

"You should see the snow fall into the sea," Goldie said.

"I've never seen the sea."

"Oh, you must, Stephen. I live in Donaghadee, which is a fishing village near Belfast. Oh, to watch the snow settle over the boats in the harbor and sweep across the gray water . . . it's lovely, really."

The snow was beautiful then, too, coming down through the huge ponderosas. We came out of the trees into a clearing where the whole world looked white.

"Stop," Goldie said.

I pulled over, though there were no other cars. Goldie got out and ran into the meadowful of snow. It was so white you couldn't tell where the hills were or how far the meadow extended into the whiteness. I didn't know what she was doing. She looked so frail, running like that into the wide expanse of nothing. It was eerie to see her fading behind the white sheen, as if the air were a deep hole and would swallow her.

I rolled down the window and called to her, but she didn't stop running.

Two months went by, right into December, and Goldie was still there. She had stopped going into town with my father. I guess she'd seen as many museums and churches as anyone could stand.

So she stayed at the trailer with me. Not that I found that a problem: By then I was used to the way she did things. When she was getting dressed, I stayed out of her way, and I developed a grudging respect for her five A.M. coffee. Sometimes I got up and watched the sunrise with her, and we all had breakfast together like ordinary people.

After my father went off to work, Goldie and I sorted out the day. Sometimes we hunted the wash. We'd go after rabbits or quail, and Goldie got so she could shoot a bird in the head from twenty-five yards. I showed her how to hold the dead birds tightly and break their skin at the breastbone so the skin and feathers peeled back like a jacket. We cleaned the quail and soaked them in salt water and made stuffing with bread and spices.

More often we just scouted the terrain. Goldie liked the desert because Ireland was cool and wet, the antithesis of the Southwest. She was fascinated how the ocotillo rolled its leaves in the dryness and the saguaros stored tons of water. We looked for animals— coatis, javelinas, snakes. She seemed to see things more quickly than I, maybe because the land was new to her. She picked out a stock-still deer on the hillside, an eagle sitting on rocks with a rocky background.

"Do you think we could see a mountain lion?" she asked.

"Not in daytime."

"I'd like awfully to see one."

"They're here," I said, "but they hunt at night."

That night she begged my father to take her to look for a mountain lion.

"A puma? Hah! We wouldn't have the chance of a pimp at St. Peter's to see a mountain lion."

"Stephen says they're around."

"Oh, they're around. But they don't want to see you."

"We could drive the back roads," Goldie said. "Don't they hunt at night?"

"No way," my father said. He smiled patiently and pinched her arm, and every night for two weeks after that, they drove the back roads over in the Papago Reservation.

Something happened on these excursions. When they returned late at night my father looked haggard and drawn, and he'd sit down and have a stiff shot of rye whiskey. He wasn't angry or short with me or Goldie. He'd talk normally, but I could tell the trip had exhausted him in a way that was beyond just the driving. At first I thought it was burning the candle late and early. My father wasn't used to staying up late and getting up at five. But it was more than that.

The next night, just as they were about to leave, I asked whether I could go along. "Do you mind?" I asked Goldie.

"You don't want to go," my father said.

"Why don't I?"

"You don't."

But he wouldn't give a reason, and Goldie didn't mind, so I went. She sat between us in the front seat, and nothing much happened on the paved road over to the reservation. When we turned off, though, Goldie sat forward. She braced her hands on the dash and pressed her face close to the windshield. We proceeded slowly, thirty miles an hour or so, the speed at which Goldie said she could see best. The headlights jerked over mesquite and saguaro and cholla, and some-times we ran without a bend in the track for ten miles or more toward some village whose name was no name—Vamori, Idak, Gu Oidak.

All the while Goldie talked. The silhouette of her glassy forehead and her arced nose and mouth blurred against the splayed light that moved in front of the truck, but she spoke without a pause, in that lilting voice. She recounted incidents from her childhood in Dona-ghadee. Her father was a fisherman, her mother a baker. They had a small house, old it was, she said, down at the rocks. She had got a scholarship to school, the first of her family to go away. They had all been fishermen laboring over nets and boats. . .

I gradually began to feel the cloudy days over Goldie's sea, and to see the long sloping green farms bordered by gray stone walls. And I felt my father sink down gently behind the wheel.

We saw kangaroo rats, badgers, snakes, deer. Once a coyote crossed the track in front of the lights. But there were no mountain lions.

Not long after that my father stopped taking Goldie on those late rides. He said it was the expense of the gas; and finding a mountain lion was against all odds. But I understood it was something else which troubled him. He had come up against something he'd never faced before, which was what to do next. He liked Goldie. She was the first woman he'd cared about since my mother, or maybe ever, but she was a strain on him, too. Normally he was the one in control, the person to say yes or no to things, but with Goldie he found himself the one holding on. At dinner he'd stare at her, not listening to her talk, but looking at her as if he were trying to figure out something. From what I could tell, Goldie was satisfied with her life. She had no plans to leave. But the idea of her leaving was always there in the air like a hawk circling, throwing its shadow across the ground.

It was about this time, too, that I went to see George White Foot. He was on the last half hour of his shift at the Safeway over on Speedway, and when I first got a glimpse of him—black hair in a pony tail, tall, slouched over the end of one of the checkout stands, he looked as though he were moving in slow motion.

"Hey, George," I said.

"If it isn't Steve White Feet," he said. "What you got, man?"

His eyes were glazed, and I could tell he was operating on batteries. "I was going to buy a six-pack," I said. "What kind do you like?"

"Anything."

I bought a double-pack of Miller and waited in the truck. When George finished, we drove out Tanque Verde. All along the highway huge divots had been scoured in the saguaro and greasewood for new houses. While one crew scraped the hillside, another was erecting frames for the families that would settle there.

"It makes you wonder, doesn't it?" I said.

"Wonder what?" George stared straight ahead.

"Look at the houses. Where's the water coming from?"

George wasn't paying attention to the houses. He was swilling beer and staring through the neon lights. "I'm going to Safford next week," he said. "Are you done out there yet with your old man?"

"Not yet."

"Shit," George said in a disgusted voice. Then he softened. "It's not bad pay. The union takes an interest."

"I'm not a copper miner," I said.

"Neither am I."

I imagined the daylight breaking across the huge orange copper pit, and men filing one at a time through a metal gate. All day they would chew the earth with huge machines, then go home and come back the next day. At the end of the week, they'd have money.

"You got to do something, Steve," George said.

He looked at me, but his eyes were blank. "Give yourself a break," I told him. "You don't have to go."

"A break? Like you? Give myself a break like you? At least I see my chances when they come at me. I got to jump."

"Jump where?"

"Fuck you," George said. He turned away and swigged the beer. He was afraid, that was all. But he wasn't afraid of Safford. He was afraid of the same thing I was: the dark land up ahead and beyond the headlights where the highway went on into nothing.

In January my father became more distant, as if he were edging away from us. I didn't notice it at first because it was a gradual shift, and day-to-day things didn't change much. He was often late for dinner—that's what I remember—and I began to wonder whether he was working late or going drinking or what.

One night Goldie and I had prepared a rabbit with gravy and rice and a nice salad. She'd dressed up for the occasion in a Mexican skirt and blouse she'd bought in Nogales as a souvenir, and she'd fixed her hair with turquoise pins. She'd put on perfume, too, which she seldom wore.

We were drinking Coors to tide us over, watching out the kitchen window at the gray dusk sliding down from the mountains. I was conscious how soft her skin looked above the scalloped neckline of her blouse, how her bare neck curved so delicately from her rounded shoulders. Her cheeks were flushed from the beer and from the heat of the rabbit's cooking.

"Where is he, do you think?" she asked.

"Looking for mountain lions."

She smiled but did not look at me. "They must be in caves all through these hills."

I nodded. The land out the window had faded. The Sierritas were lavender and blue, ebbing toward black, and in the yard the arc light had come on.

"You'd look for a mountain lion for me, wouldn't you, Stephen?"

"I would," I said.

She laughed and stood up and twirled around in the small space of the kitchen. Then she stopped and looked back out the window. "Do you know what he's really doing?"

"No."

"You do."

"He's looking for a place in town," I said.

Goldie seemed surprised. "What place?"

"Somewhere better than the trailer. He wants it for you."

We were silent for a long time, and the small space tightened up. Goldie didn't move from the window.

"Are you going to stay with him?" I asked.

That was the only time Goldie didn't say anything. She looked around at me with an expression so pained I couldn't move.

"Let's drink," she said finally. "The Irish are famous for drinking."

She got out the whiskey bottle from under the sink and poured two glasses and gave me one. Then she went into the living room.

A moment later, I heard the door open and close, and the trailer was silent.

That was when I knew how my mother had lived through all those years. I felt at that moment the weight of an emptiness of love, the terrible absence which wanted filling. Momentum, it seemed to me, was like wind seeking and seeking: even when it was invisible it was there, driving forward, unable to be calm. I held my breath for a minute, then I followed Goldie.

I stood on the landing. Goldie was in the yard, illuminated by the arc light, holding her glass of whiskey above her head. She swirled through the light, lifting her skirt with one hand, twirling like a dancer across the gravel. She paused and drank and continued toward the rim of the trail into the sandwash.

"Stephen," she said. "Come on."

But she didn't wait for me. Her voice carried through the stillness and then she was gone over the edge and into the ravine.

I glanced down the dirt road toward the highway hoping to see the headlights of my father's truck sweeping up among the saguaros. But there was nothing but the vacant dark highway and the barely perceptible ridge of hills.

I went after Goldie, not knowing what else to do. By the time I reached the sandy wash, she had started upstream. Her dark tracks curved through the sand and around the first bend, and I called to her and heard my own voice echo against the rocks.

I knew she was waiting for me. I walked slowly, feeling my steps yield to the soft sand.

She was there, around that first outcropping of rocks. Her white blouse was vivid in the air. She had taken the turquoise pins from her hair, and it fell across her shoulder like black feathers.

I stopped and waited.

"Come here, Stephen," she said.

I went closer.

"Smell my hair." She bent her head so that her black hair cascaded into her hand, and she held it up to me.

I breathed in. She pushed her hair into my face, across my cheek. Her hair smelled of apricot.

"Smell here," she said. "What does my skin smell like?" She pulled her blouse down over one shoulder.

"Cholla blossoms."

"Close your eyes."

I closed my eyes.

"Tight," she said.

I kept my eyes tightly closed, feeling my heart beat different colors behind the lids. The breeze smoothed across my damp forehead. In the thicket not far away, thrashers and quail were settling in. I heard the swishing of Goldie's skirt, the movement of cloth, the sigh she made when the cool air touched her bare skin.

In the early morning, while my father and Goldie were still sleeping, I packed the few things I had and coasted the truck out of the yard. About a mile down, I abandoned the truck where the sand gully intersected the gravel. It would take my father a while to understand, then at least an hour to reach the truck. I walked from there to the Sasabe road, and sometime toward dawn got a ride north from a Mexican businessman. A Papago took me west on the main road to Sells, and by evening I was in Blythe, California.

I was going somewhere where it snowed into the sea—Northern California or maybe Oregon. I wasn't certain of anything. It was the beginning for me of a sadness which, I suppose, had to come to me sometime, an aching that lasted for years.

EVERY TIME I SPILL
RED WINE I PANIC

by Stratis Haviaras

Three old women in black, like the mythical *graiae* whose names meant terror, panic, and suffering, were walking ahead of me on the two-hour journey east of our village along the bay's edge toward Nauplion. They were carrying bread and clean shirts for their sons, held by the Germans in a sixteenth-century fort, the Promontory of Acronauplia. One of the three women was my maternal grandmother. Two weeks before, a detachment of the German army, accompanied by several masked informers from the area, had encircled and combed the plain of Argos, capturing and identifying two dozen or so men who were listed as members of the underground. My father was one of the prisoners. The previous week my mother had gone to visit him and hadn't come back. She was nine months pregnant. We soon learned that she, too, had been detained by the Germans.

My grandmother had refused to take me along, saying that a two-hour journey on foot would be too much for my age. It was June 28, 1944, my ninth birthday.

I disobeyed her and, counting on her poor vision, followed her and the other two at a distance.

We had started off before sunrise, and now the three women had reached the halfway mark, the chapel of Prophet Elias, where they paused for prayer and a few minutes of rest. I stepped down from the dirt road and put my feet in the water. I had no shoes, and although the soles of my feet had hardened in the past two years, the pebbles and the salt that had washed over the sea-level path made travel on foot painful.

My grandparents had come from Greek settlements in Asia Minor. In 1912, uprooted by the Turks, they had emigrated to the United States, but at the end of World War I were allowed to return to their homeland, which they did, only to be caught in the second slaughter in ten years by the Turks. The Greeks and Armenians who survived made their way to Greece, and in 1925 both sides of my family found shelter in a refugee settlement near the swampy estuary of the River Erassinos. Three hectares of farming land per family, a vegetable cannery, and small-time fishing in the bay comprised the subsistence economy of the new village. Malaria, typhus, and tuberculosis were the names of death in that time.

We lived on meager harvests of vegetables, most of which were absorbed at production prices by the local cannery. In his spare time, my father earned extra income as a house painter. Although he had no schooling, he was a refined man, and a journal that he left behind contained drawings, meditations, stories, and entries on cinematography, at a time when there was not even electricity in the village (it came in the 1960s, thanks to a native son who had done well in shipping).

At the age of nine I could remember having seen my father no more than three times. If I made it all the way to Acronauplia, this would be the fourth.

The first time had been when he was released from political detention, so that he could be sent to the Italian front in Albania. I saw him in a tavern in a uniform, drinking wine with friends. He told me to go home.

The second time was at the end of that war, just days before the German invasion and his going into hiding.

And the third time was the previous September, when one evening he showed up in the field that my mother and I farmed. He was armed with a rifle, and his clothes hadn't been washed for a long time. My father asked me to go to the village and buy some wine. Reluctantly, my mother rinsed a bottle and handed it to me, saying, Be careful! I knew the way. But not at night, not with jackals roaming the nearly dry riverbed halfway to the village, and not during the curfew. I said, I'll be careful.

It must have been eight-thirty; the country roads were already empty, the riverbed strangely quiet and darkened, and the village deserted. The tavern, the same tavern I'd seen my father drinking in before the war, had already closed. So far I had not run into any German sentries. I went straight to the tavernkeeper's house and said to him, I want this bottle filled with red wine. His wife said, No! He himself stared at me blankly, as if I must not know the seriousness of the curfew. Who sent you, anyway, he said. I handed him the bottle. He went to the basement, filled it up, and handed it back to me, saying, No money. It's all right.

I walked out of the village quietly and fast. It was dark enough for anyone to become lost, but I knew my way by heart, and in a few minutes was stepping down to the riverbed where the jackals now waited. They were howling at the top of their lungs, waiting for somebody to cross, the smaller the better. Halt! I heard, but it was far away. I wasn't concerned. The three most important things now were my father, the wine, and the jackals. Seeing nothing at all in the pitch black night and hearing only the hungry beasts scared me more than anything else. But I didn't lose my direction. I knew where my father was, how to get there, to deliver the wine and feel his hand resting lightly on my shoulder.

What an unusual man he was, my father, in those painful days. His calm voice, his warm, light complexion. Average height now, but rather tall then; well-built, but by no means athletic; fair-to-reddish hair; clear blue-gray eyes. Thin-lipped, he would smile without showing his straight, white teeth. I loved him although I hadn't seen or known much of him, and I feared him because he lived in danger, and I feared something might happen to him. But the aura about him had instilled in me the faith that what he did would stop the killing and suffering, and that bread and better days would come back to us for good once the Germans and their hirelings were gone.

Holding the bottle to my chest and crying loudly, I began to cross the riverbed. The jackals, instead of leaping at me, began to growl and to tear at each other. I ran, hit my toes on a stone, and fell, but as I fell I raised the hand holding the bottle, saving the wine. As I found later, the nail of my left big toe had come off and I was bleeding there.

When I reached the east bank a voice met me: Don't cry, cousin, you're doing all right. It was so dark that when his load of firewood scraped my face I still couldn't see him. But the voice did belong to an older cousin of mine.

So where were you five minutes ago? I shouted at him, outraged that he hadn't shown up when I really needed help.

He said the jackals weren't as near as I thought. But the truth is he had decided to sit down and wait awhile before he ventured to cross the riverbed. As I took the footpath to our field, still crying loudly, I heard the voice of another man who I knew had been dead since the year before, who used to carry firewood on his back just like my cousin. His widow and five children were the poorest in the village, but one evening I happened to be in their house at dinnertime, and although their entire meal was a bowl of dandelion greens without oil or salt, they asked me to join them at the table. We crossed ourselves and the widow asked God to bless the dinner, but the amount of food on the table didn't increase. The widow said that she and the children could hear her husband's voice speaking to them in the evening, advising them to share their food with others who were hungry, and always to have some wine in the house.

My father was glad about the wine, but it was too dark for me to see in his eyes the pride he felt for me. My mother helped me wash, bandaged my toe, and put me to bed. It must have been that night that she got pregnant.

The months after September rushed by. My father became a member of the political arm of the Resistance, and though he traveled from village to village, expanding the network, he hardly ever stopped by ours. Now I was going to pay him a visit.

Three old women in black, three crows named Terror, Panic, and Suffering . . . carrying food for the dead. Silent in their detached blacknesses, blighting the view of the citadel of ancient Tirins to the east. To the west were the gates of Nauplion. Rail tracks, empty streets, strong light and shadow. And the rest of the city a bold brush stroke as I ran to catch up with the three old ones who'd already begun to climb up the hill toward the fortress of Acronauplia.

I'm with them, I said to the German guard at the gate, pointing at the grandmothers who had gone through, but when I caught up with them they were not the least surprised to see me. In the prison yard there were as many as two hundred men, lying down injured in head or limb or peering down at the choppy sunlight crusting the bay. The old ones went one way and I another, looking at faces: faces resigned and sleepy, looking blankly down at the deep water, looking but seeing nothing. One face was smiling. My father had spotted me first but waited until I saw him.

How are you? How are things at home, he said. The left side of his head was bandaged and blood had seeped through the dressing covering his ear.

I felt my shoulders rising like wings with goose bumps above them. I don't remember what I said.

You're going to have to take things into your own hands from now on, he said, resting his hand on my shoulder.

I didn't know where to start.

You'll have to figure everything out for yourself, he said, and already he was turning away from me to have a word or two with Grandmother. And what he told her was that my mother had lost the child in a forced abortion and had been sent on a train to Germany. Also that my mother had tried to sign for him to be sent to Germany as well. He had found out, argued with her, and had refused to board the train.

I didn't know what to make of that, and the grandmothers were no help whatever. I remember being glad that my father had chosen not to go so far away.

Three weeks later my grandmother and I got up before dawn, and after walking for about an hour arrived at a railroad stop to meet the Nauplion–Corinth train. Every car was packed with prisoners, and my father was supposed to be among them, but we never found him, never saw him. The train left and we stayed behind, and it took us two hours to make it home. Later that morning, outside the city of Corinth, in a field called Negri's, thirty prisoners, my father among them, were executed by the Germans and buried in a mass grave.

Everyone knew this except me. My grandmother lied to me, and the neighbors respected her wish to keep it secret. She told me instead that my father had escaped from Corinth and had joined the armed ones on the mountain.

After the war he will come home, as your mother certainly will, so you won't end up in the orphanage, she said. I had no reason to believe otherwise.

From that day I began to search for my father. I looked at thousands of faces under the clouds. Every stranger, every soldier regardless of camp. And when the Germans retreated and the informers of the Germans took off their masks and became generals, ministers, and mayors, I looked at their faces, too.

It wasn't until two years later that I found out the truth, after my mother returned from the concentration camp and told me that my father had died, killed by Nazi bullets in Corinth. He's dead, she said. Your father is not among us. The Germans shot him along with twenty-nine others. Their families are trying to raise funds now for a memorial . . .

She explained in detail and I understood, but I never really believed her. She said, You'll have to be in charge from now on. I knew all about that. But I couldn't stop looking for him in the faces of soldiers and strangers. And the kindest among them would ask me questions, and I would tell them I am looking for my father, it's been three years since I last saw him: gray eyes, fair-to-reddish complexion, a warm voice that keeps advising me, Do not steal, do not waste, be truthful, be generous to others because if they don't survive, you won't survive either.

And even at the dedication of the memorial I was looking for him in the crowd. We were in a small cemetery, and the memorial was a four-meter-tall marble obelisk, bearing the names of the fallen and a brief inscription: GREECE'S HONORABLE SONS . . . I can't remember the rest; I was busy looking for him.

In 1967, when the last generation of Nazi collaborators took over the government in Athens, the army made plans to expand an artillery base near the small cemetery, and it promptly moved the dead and the monuments to an undisclosed location.

In order perhaps to prove that my father was just another victim of circumstance, post-war Germany offered us a sum of money as part of war reparations, but we were never given a chance to throw the money into their faces. Our own government kept the funds. Poor father. Poor, poor father. At age twelve I went to work, and for the next twenty years I supported myself and what was left of the family as a construction worker. That's how I understood taking things into my own hands.

Freedom? It has its price, my father would have said, the price being sacrifice and perhaps an obscure death. I left Greece in 1967, shortly after the military takeover of the government. By that time I had looked at every Greek face and I knew my father was no longer among them. I left, but I am still looking at faces, searching for radiance, intelligence, trust, the dream of love, and the promise of freedom. And every time I spill red wine I panic.

Be generous with your life, I hear his voice advising me. But although my heart leaps at the sound of his voice, I soon turn away from it, the way I turn away from the voices of those who betrayed and killed him.

Be prudent, I advise myself.

My father was executed at the age of thirty-four. I hardly knew him, and now I don't even know where his bones are resting. A lost son, my only son—that's how he feels to me now, when I am old enough to be his father.

CONTACT

by John N. Cole

That rambling, shingled house had five chimneys, brick, painted white except for the single topmost course. That was black, a thin, jet line that gave definition to each of the pale and graceful arms that rose above the roofs of the several wings like arms reaching for the clouds. That outermost house on a slim finger of sand extended precariously between the open Atlantic and a brackish lake was the essence of summer romance, even without those five white chimneys rising. Surrounded by a wooden wall that was shingled like the house and topped with curves and pillars capped with white trim, a garden bloomed at the southeast corner. Along the long west side, rosa rugosa dropped pink and lavender petals on a green, green lawn, its edges sharply sculpted once every week by Jimmy, the gnarled, dark Italian gardener whose broken English always made our grandmother smile.

At that lawn's western rim a carefully crafted wooden bulkhead disciplined the lake, edged there with cattails. On the late spring day my brother Chick and I climbed to the peak of the roof that rose above our room, we stood next to the tall chimney sprung from the dining room fireplace far below. With our sneakered boys' feet braced on either side of the roof's sloping peak, and with a reassuring hand pressed against the chimney's warm flank, we surveyed a landscape as enchanting as any illustrated fantasy found in the pages of *Treasure Island, The Last of the Mohicans, A Tale of Two Cities,* or any of the other handsome books that our father had made certain were in our library and in our memories. More romance. But romance surpassed by the view from our rooftop.

First, the lake, brighter blue than the sky swept clean by a northwest breeze, then across the lake to the young greens and sudden browns of the Talmadge farm after his plow's early prying into winter-sealed fields. And beyond the farm the darker green sea of pines and scrub oak that swelled west to become the Northwest Woods, a place we knew only as horizon, the place that framed the gossamer sunsets we watched each evening from the bedroom below us that we shared, Chick and I, sleeping each in our separate beds but close, side by side, as we had, so close to each other, ever since he was born just sixteen months after my arrival.

In those beds after the sunset, as the night brought us visions of Uncas and Long John Silver, we often felt the tremors of breaking waves falling hard on the packed sand of the ribbon of beach that bordered the dunes just to our east. Swells born in a squall off Dakar rolled west from Africa to meet the northwest wind fresh from the Talmadge farm, a wind that sharpened those seas dulled by distance, brought them to attention, standing tall so when they fell they toppled like some great emerald tower crashing on the sand as our beds trembled in the dark.

We had each other more than we had anyone, or anyone had us. Our mother, Helen, traveled the world with friends. Our father's office was in the city and his country weekends were white flannels for tennis and white dinner jackets for dinner parties under the summer stars. At the far southwest end of the house, in a low-roofed, modestly chimneyed, single chamber that had once been a small cottage on the farm my grandmother had bought three decades before, she had her quarters. Emma Darrow, Yankee lady, married first to Charles Dodd, tubercular collector of gold coins and butterflies, and heir to the Dodd estate. When he died young, that estate became Emma's, who married again and used the money to add twenty more rooms, four more chimneys, and a second story to the farmer's cottage by the lake.

Emma shared that house generously with her daughter, Helen,

who had married my father when she was just eighteen, and Emma saw to it that the grandchildren's wing was built, with that high-ceilinged boys' room with its built-in toy chests and bookcases where my brother's bed and mine were moored like two skiffs along the southwest wall, afloat on a great sweep of maple floor.

Alone together most of our days, with no one there to turn misfortune off course, Chick and I survived merely because misfortune never sailed our way. We lived our summer splendors protected by the elemental innocence that safeguards kittens and dandelions. Being the older, at twelve, I led each of our excursions, just as I had stepped from the porch, clung to a window ledge, found a toehold on the gable that sloped from our bathroom, and pulled myself past the gutter onto the shingled roof that led up to the chimney where Chick joined me on that late spring morning when we stood together, feeling the heartbeats of freedom under the fronts of our matching Saks Fifth Avenue short-sleeved summer shirts, and contemplated the mysteries of the distant Northwest Woods.

"Boys! Boys! What are you doing up there?"

Our grandmother's soprano recalibrated our observations; we focused on the green lawn at our feet, just beyond the white railing of the porch below us. Emma was there, her housecoat rippling in the breeze off the lake, a breeze that twitched the graying tendrils of her uncombed morning hair. Thrilled that our ascent had been noted, swept by a surge of even more reckless exhibition, we both waved with both hands, teetered with intended wavering on the roof peak, and laughed like crows cawing from a treetop.

Emma was not amused. Even in the thin air of our stratosphere, we sensed her outrage. "Get down from there! Get down from there this minute," she called, the volume of her high voice stirring nesting red-wing blackbirds from the cattails. "You boys get down from there and go straight to your room. You do that right now or I'll call the police."

Smiling at each other, pleased with the attention we had generated, Chick and I climbed down, swung from the roof's edge and dropped to the porch, opened a screen door, and went inside. If we went to our room, it was only for a moment. The rest of the day we spent on the beach, building sand forts at the Atlantic's dancing edge—forts sacrificed to an implacable rising tide that crumbled parapets and destroyed defenses with gratifying disregard for the lives of every imagined defender.

Our father was sitting on the front porch, smoking one of his Chesterfield cigarettes, when Chick and I walked up the flagstone path to the house, swinging our damp, sandy towels. He had driven down from the city and had already changed to his white flannel trousers.

We both knew he was waiting for us, but we were uncertain why. The episode of six hours before had left no footprint on our consciousness.

He was a large man, big-chested, broad-shouldered, a man whose body had to be a presence in each of his days. Unmonitored, that body could race toward obesity and become a burden—one reason for our father's allegiance to squash and tennis. The other reasons were more complex. Above the broad shoulders his remarkable head rose like a domed temple. A bald head somehow made more imposing by its baldness, and dominated by the swirling darkness of two burning, deep-brown eyes. The eyes turned directly at me and Chick.

"Miss Emma phoned me in the city," he said, his slow speech touched with the accents of the Old South. "She said you boys were on the roof, the roof she just had shingled."

Leaning back in his chair, our father inhaled smoke from his cigarette, tilted forward, and asked, "Boys, is that true?" As he spoke, smoke drifted and curled from his lips with each ominous word.

When I nodded yes, he sighed a long, long sigh, a sigh born in the fields of a small North Carolina tobacco town, a sigh that spanned past dreams and present realities and swirled in the mists of both. Through the wash of memory he realized a moment had overtaken him, come galloping through time to crystallize that past and present, to sweep aside routine and move him and his two sons into uncharted waters on a voyage he had not planned, across dark emotional seas toward an uncertain destination.

That voyage had begun for him a quarter century before. At nineteen, the oldest surviving son of a family of nine brothers and sisters—a family left fatherless by the early death of our Methodist minister grandfather—our father shouldered the obligations of leadership and support. He rode to the Winston-Salem railroad station in the back of a tobacco wagon and took the next train to New York City, the only place within his ken where he believed enough money could be made to sustain himself, his mother, and his siblings.

He left behind a life—a way of life—and that leaving lasted forever. Our father maintained a yearning for the South, a love of Dixie, that region of cotton, tobacco, darkies, Uncle Remus, Brer Rabbit, My Old Kentucky Home, and the parish of a minister who lived at the edge of a green patchwork of tobacco fields, tobacco barns, tobacco auctions, and tobacco towns at the very center of the world's largest single tobacco harvest. Our father had grown up a farm boy, bare feet dark with red clay, his head and heart nourished with fundamental rural truths: Idleness is sin, work is the way to salvation, loyalty is prime, family comes first.

Virtues in the fields around Winston-Salem became charming anomalies in the drawing rooms of Manhattan. Carrying entrées from the Duke family, already tobacco royalty and, fortunately for our father, also Methodists, the tall, dark and undeniably handsome young man from the South was quick to comprehend the sparks he struck with Park Avenue Yankees when he sang "Swing Low, Sweet Chariot" and "Carry Me Back to Old Virginny" at penthouse dinner parties. He became one of those people who are adopted by Society with a capital S. Eligible, well-mannered, and above all absolutely and so charmingly Southern, he began to be invited to more dinners, more receptions, more opening nights, more masquerade balls, and then to spend entire country weekends at estates with swimming pools and private tennis courts.

Which is how and why he became an excellent dancer and a tournament class tennis player: talents that were fail-safe footholds in a precarious and brittle world—a world light years from the back of a tobacco wagon.

Arrived at a Southampton costume party dressed as a gypsy organ grinder, complete with hand-cranked organ, golden earring, and a live and ill-mannered monkey on a leash, he was introduced to

Helen Dodd, then seventeen, innocent in every sense of the word and quite taken aback by the attentions of a man she considered an entertainer, not a guest, and therefore not to be acknowledged with more than polite reserve and defensive generalities.

The next morning the doorbell rang at that house by the lake. When the maid answered she was told by the large man with dark eyes that he had come to call on Miss Helen. That information, relayed first to Emma and then to Helen, brought both to a guest room window where they could peer through at the front porch without being seen.

"Why it's the organ grinder," Helen said, blushing at the embarrassment of seeing a tradesman at the front door and wondering how on earth the gypsy had discovered where she lived.

"Stay here," Emma ordered. "I'll take care of him," with hard emphasis on the final pronoun.

It was one of the few times in her life that Emma's will failed to conquer. Her daughter and the man from Winston-Salem were married before the year ended, in the cavernous, Byzantine extravagance of St. Bartholomew's Church on Park Avenue, complete with photograph in the *Times* and the Sunday *Tribune*'s rotogravure, and capped with a first-class Cunard cabin heading for Paris, Cairo, and Rome. The tobacco field boy had become a man of the world.

A man of two worlds. Our father never loosened his ties to the South. No amount of diligent Yankee society could persuade him to relinquish his okra, his Mason-Dixon idioms: "darky . . . y'all . . . Miss Emma . . . yes sir . . . no sir . . . 'cuz . . . pickaninny . . . Mammy . . ." and each of the rest of the Southern signatures that tagged the slowly spoken language of his years.

But he paid other high prices in pure emotional coin to his new world. In addition to the concerts, the clubs, the dinner parties, the endless array of afternoon cocktails, he came to accept the then fashionable notion that servants managed both households and children. Sons and daughters, in those times, were turned over to nannies and mam'selles as routinely as breakfast, lunch, and dinner were delegated to the head cook, or shopping trips to the chauffeur.

This was a price refined from our father's deepest emotional ore.

His values embraced family, reveled in the social mingling of the kitchen, and above all, welcomed the loving disorder of children. Even as he recalled the easy intimacies of a tumultuous family raised under the single roof of a Southern farmhouse, our father's own years as a parent were lived at the cool remove imposed by social mores of a society he had married, but never understood. Each of his years of luxurious living was painfully stressed by the life he knew he was missing.

There, on that porch on that late spring evening, there with his two sons standing thin in their swimming trunks before him, he made his decision to reach for what he had missed. And, because there were so many years gone, and so many more ahead, he knew the encounter needed to be complete and unfettered. Helen was in Salzburg, Miss Emma had returned to her distant quarters; our father was alone with his two sons.

"Boys," he said, the words as slow as time, "I'm going to have to give you a licking. You must learn to behave." The dark eyes trained their intensity on ours. "You knew better, didn't you?"

Unable to muster a voice, we both nodded. In each of our skulls the word "licking" reverberated, an express train tumbling through the tunnel of our imagination. Our father had never laid a hand on us; indeed, he had scarcely spoken. And now we were pledged a licking. We were stunned by visions of our violent future.

"You boys get dressed," our father said, "and we'll go out for dinner." Stunned again. Another first. Chick and I walked down that long hall to our room sharing the silence of the condemned, but exchanging quizzical looks, tentative half smiles, and the mutual shrugs that told us we were equally baffled, and equally afraid.

Dinner was at a roadhouse restaurant, an unpretentious, sprawling place on the main highway, a place where local Rotarians gathered for luncheon meetings on Monday, and returned separately with their wives and families on Saturday nights—not a place where my father was likely to meet any of his tennis friends from the club. The food was fine, and there was a great deal of it: men's food, steaks, chops, and roast beef.

Chick and I could not finish our meal. That licking stuck in our craw, would not let go of our uneasy anticipations. But our father tried hard to dispel our anxieties. He told stories of his own youth, moralized a bit about how the constancy of chores kept his boyhood relatively trouble free, and remembered his own mother and father with smiles and rural details of that Winston-Salem life lived in such a different time and place. He was, for the first time, trying to give his sons a portrait of his past.

Next morning, as new sunbeams climbed our room's pale walls, our father, shaved and dressed, his white flannels as perfect as the new day, opened our bedroom door. "Let's go, boys," he said. We pulled on shirts and shorts, rubbed the grit from our eyes, and followed him along the long hall, down the stairs, out the front door, across the flagstones, past the shingled garden wall, and along the road's edge until we came to the vast emptiness of an eight-car garage built at the height of the opulent optimism of the early twenties. At its far end were the chauffeur's quarters, vacant on that preseason morning.

Opening the door to the small suite of rooms, our father sat on the edge of a worn sofa. "You wait outside," he told me. "Chick, you come in here." Swinging from his hand as he motioned was his razor strop, a wide length of hard leather that usually hung next to the sink in our father's bathroom. Each morning it was pulled horizontal from its hook and became a smooth surface stroked by one of the seven matched-set, ebony-handled straight razors that had been one of our father's many wedding gifts.

When Chick walked in, our father closed the door. I could hear the leather strike, and tried to count the times. There was no other sound and soon the door opened and Chick came out, his eyes swimming in tears.

Then I went in and the door closed. "Take down your pants," our father told me, "and put your hands on the windowsill." The strop rose and fell, perhaps four times. I bit my lip to stifle sound, but, like Chick's, my eyes filled.

Our father opened the door, and motioned Chick inside. "I hope," he began, but then stopped, his own eyes suddenly awash as tears streamed along his freshly shaven cheeks. A terrible sob racked him, his chest and shoulders spasmed with frightening intensity. Mute, he extended his arms, his eyes telling us to come. Once within his grasp, both of us were pulled to that broad, heaving chest and clutched there while our father wept for the sons he hardly knew, the life he had left so long ago, and the new life he lived so relentlessly.

At last the terrible sounds subsided.

"I love you," he said, hoarse. "You remember that."

And, after a while, the three of us walked out into the sun.

That was the first and last time our father embraced us. Not wars, my brother's death, or even our father's own imminent end prompted more such awesome intimacy.

There was, for Chick and me, just that single contact.

BUCK FEVER

by Laton McCartney

Every month my father would bring home a new batch of outdoor magazines—*Field & Stream, Outdoor Life, Sports Afield*—that he'd read in an evening's sitting, a stiff highball always in hand, and then pass along to me.

As an adolescent, my own tastes ran more to comic books and adventure magazines with their tales of lost treasure and explorers who were held captive by scantly clad Amazons. Yet we lived on a remote cattle ranch in Wyoming where reading matter was in short supply, so I'd eagerly devour Pappy's magazines from cover to cover, turning first to the stories, my favorites, about fathers and sons who hunted and fished together.

Invariably, I noticed, these narratives sounded common themes. For one thing, you could be sure that the boy would learn an important lesson during these outings, thereby taking a giant step on the road to manhood. Typically, too, Dad would be reminded at some point in the story that there were few things more important in life then taking his kid bass fishing or deer hunting. And despite the generation gap and whatever differences they had at home, father and son always emerged from these trips the best of pals.

Reading these stories I first began to suspect that life didn't necessarily imitate art. At least not my life. My own father was a "man's man," a hard-drinking, Yale-educated cattle rancher who was a world-class fly fisherman and a crack shot. Pappy had hunted brown and Kodiak bear in Alaska, killed a jaguar in a Brazilian jungle, shot mountain sheep in Canada, wild boar in Arkansas, and downed countless elk, antelope, deer, duck, and Canada geese. When he wasn't hunting, he was fishing. The walls of the den, his darkly paneled inner sanctum, were hung with a near record sailfish from the Gulf Stream, trophy trout from all over the West, and the mounted heads and horns of a goodly number of God's wild creatures.

Yet this passion for the sporting life was not something my father willingly shared with me, his only son. From the time I reached adolescence to the day I went east to college, we hunted and fished together no more than a half dozen times.

In retrospect, I think Pappy felt this neglect on his part was really an act of compassion. Early on, my father had decided I was afflicted with what he called "buck fever." As Pappy defined it, buck fever was the antithesis of grace under fire, Hemingway's characterization of courage. Put a rifle or a fly rod in my hands, and I'd invariably choke, especially if there was a deer in my scope or a fat brown trout supping on the evening hatch and my father happened to be in the vicinity.

No point in making a child who was tone deaf study music, or demanding that an offspring who suffered from vertigo climb mountains. No point in trying to mold Murph, as Pappy called me, into an outdoorsman. My father simply gave up on me, wrote me off like a bad debt.

I loved my father. I loved the smell of his pipe, the sound of his deep infectious laughter as he listened to the Jack Benny show on Sunday nights, and the outrageous practical jokes he played on his friends. Sober he was all charm and generosity, a rakishly handsome Peck's bad boy whom women frequently found irresistible and men admired. At his best, he reminded me of the hero of a Zane Grey novel: a valiant, straight-shooting son of the Old West.

But when he drank he was mean as a rattlesnake. Several times a year, he got into brutal barroom fights in Laramie, or Rock River, a little town west of the ranch. And once in Denver, he'd broken the jaw of a drunk who'd sprayed seltzer down the front of my mother's dress. The drunk was the son of a prominent Denver businessman, and my father had to pay all the man's medical expenses. My grand-mother, who strongly disapproved of her only son and his drinking, said Pappy was lucky not to have gone to jail.

At home, my father could be a terror, particularly during the winter when the ranch work slackened and he had little to do except sit around the house and drink. If I said the wrong thing at the dinner table, or even looked at my father the wrong way, he'd belt me across the mouth with the back of his hand and send me sprawling. God forbid my sister, Dillon, or I woke him from his nap. He'd emerge from the bedroom, his eyes red from sleep and the copious quantities of bourbon he'd consumed at lunch, and chase us around the house like an ogre from some frightening children's fable. "I'm going to skin you two alive with a dull butter knife!" he'd threaten as we ran outside. Fortunately, he was usually too hung over to catch us.

Once my black Lab, Lucky, woke Pappy from a siesta by barking at something in the corral, a rattlesnake perhaps. Wearing his under-shorts, my father opened the bedroom door, with such force that it almost flew off the hinges, grabbed one of his hunting rifles, and called the dog from the front porch. As Lucky came running, Pappy blew off the top of his head with a 30.06.

Even my father's most ardent defenders, my mother among them ("That's the liquor talking and not your father," she'd tell Dillon and me), admitted that Pappy could be a certifiable son of a bitch and the worst kind of bully when he'd downed the odd quart of Cabin Still. Yet it took me years to get over my guilt at not being a chip off the old block, and to recognize that my propensity to choke up, this so-called buck fever of mine, stemmed from my old man and not some genetic defect or deep-seated character flaw within myself.

Granted, I was not exactly the son Pappy would have chosen if he could have custom-ordered a kid. I was a quiet, introverted boy who liked to read and draw and collect arrowheads and baseball cards. In Pappy's view I was too much of a dreamer, too lacking in aggression to deal with the harsh realities of life. "I wish Murph would hurry up and develop balls," I heard him complain to my mother when I was ten.

In an effort to toughen me up, Pappy initiated a strict regimen that had us Indian wrestling every night before dinner. The two of us would stand toe to toe and strain (or so my father would pretend) to throw the other off balance. He also gave me lessons in self-defense. In a garden-variety fistfight, my objective, Pappy explained, was to strike my adversary in the Adam's apple, thereby blocking his windpipe and causing him to gasp for air and frequently pass out. In life-or-death struggles, my father solemnly instructed me to break my opponent's nose with a sharp downward chop of the hand and then drive the broken bone into his brain with an upward thrust of the palm. The thought of the damage I might do employing these techniques—or worse, the damage I might incur fighting someone who knew them—was so frightening that I have studiously avoided fights ever since.

When I was twelve, he announced it was time I learned to hunt and fish. I welcomed the news, hoping that Pappy and I would experience some of the father and son bonding I'd read about in *Outdoor Life*. Yet I was apprehensive about fishing or hunting with my difficult, demanding father. Several years earlier, he'd introduced me to fishing in a roundabout way, and the experience had proven an unhappy one for both of us, a harbinger of what was to come.

I remember we'd been driving back to the ranch from Denver, and my father decided to stop at Estes Park to have a drink. I was probably eight at the time. Rather than take me into the bar with him, he left me in the custody of the man who ran Troutvale, one of those places where you caught trout from a big tank using a hook, line, and bread for bait. "I'm going to leave my boy here to catch a few fish while I go across the street for a quick snort," Pappy told the Troutvale proprietor.

The quick snort turned into five or six prolonged snorts. By the time Pappy came out of the bar his features were flushed with bourbon, and I'd put a significant dent in Troutvale's rainbow population. "Jesus H. Christ!" Pappy roared when he glimpsed my catch. When the proprietor informed Pappy that he owed something like thirty dollars for the fish, a sizeable sum in the late 1940s, my father, a tightfisted Scot, turned a shade of purple I had never seen before. Angrily, he produced a wad of bills from his wallet, and lifted me bodily into the truck. "What about the fish?" I cried.

"Never mind the goddamn fish," he responded. I had thought my father would have been proud of my prodigious catch but instead he raced home over the rugged mountain roads, hitting some of the bumps so hard that I held on to the seat with both hands to keep from being bounced against the roof of the truck.

I also knew my father took his fly fishing, like his hunting, extremely seriously. For five generations the McCartneys had lived within the shadows of the Rocky Mountains. We were descendants of fur traders, frontier doctors, and cattle barons, most of whom had been fly fishermen. My paternal great-great-great-grandfather was a Scottish fur trader named Robert Stuart who discovered much of the Oregon Trail in 1812. En route across Oregon and the vast, uncharted reaches of Idaho, Wyoming, and Nebraska, Stuart and his six companions fished every chance they got, using crude flies they fashioned from tufts of deer and elk hide and the feathers of game birds.

Fly fishing, in my father's eyes, was one of the things that separated the McCartneys from the hoi polloi, the *bait* fishermen who'd come late to the West and had no respect for its finite resources. By mastering the intricacies of fly fishing, I knew I could prove myself a gentleman and a worthy member of my father's clan. Of course, if I failed . . . well, the prospect was too daunting to consider.

On the day of our initial fly fishing outing my father woke me early, and we drove over to the North Platte near Saratoga on the far side of the Medicine Bows. It must have been mid-September, because the aspen had already turned, and I remember the crisp, cool autumnal air. On the river wearing an old pair of my father's waders that were too big for me, and using a little bamboo pole, I was so tense I thought I was going to throw up on the spot. But Pappy rigged up my rod and briefly reviewed the casting techniques that we'd been practicing for several weeks in anticipation of the trip. "Okay, you're on your own, now," he said, starting upstream.

I frequently fished for brookies in the beaver dam behind our house, using worms. Fly fishing was something else entirely, an arcane ritual that was entirely foreign to me. I watched my father, his omnipresent pipe clenched between his teeth, casting with a fluid grace. He effortlessly cast his fly out thirty and forty yards, placing it precisely where he wanted, it seemed. Within minutes he'd landed a sizeable brown trout.

My own casts traveled no more than a few yards, and the more effort I put into them, the worse they got. "Remember what I told you," Pappy yelled when he saw I was having trouble. "You're taking your rod too far back."

But try as I did, I was hopeless. With almost every cast the leader, which seemed to have a perverse will of its own, got tangled. I'd spend five or ten minutes undoing the knots only to lose my fly the next time I cast—it simply disappeared from the end of the line or got caught in the branches of the cottonwoods along the banks. Then I'd spend another few minutes trying to tie a new fly on properly.

At one point I somehow hooked myself painfully in the right ear lobe, and my father, who was normally the most impatient of men, calmly waded back to me, extracted the hook from my ear, and put on a new tippet and fly. "Relax, sport," he told me. "You're trying too hard."

Finally, miraculously, I hooked a fish. "Goddamn, I got one," I shouted. I saw Pappy react with a big, generous grin, his expression turning to one of stunned disbelief as I yanked the little rainbow from the water with such force that it flew over my head and disappeared into the hay field behind me.

On the ride back my father muttered something about the first time always being difficult, but I was beyond consoling. I couldn't make up my mind whether to commit suicide or simply run away and join up with a family of bait-fishing gypsies who hopefully would accept me as one of their own.

"How was the fishing?" my mother asked brightly as we traipsed into the house. My father shook his head and poured himself an entire glass of bourbon, not bothering to add the usual club soda. "To tell the truth, I've never experienced anything quite like it," he said wearily, dropping into his favorite armchair.

After our outing on the North Platte, Pappy decided to put my development as a fly fisherman on hold and concentrate instead on bringing me along as a hunter. On a Friday afternoon in October we drove out to northeastern Colorado through fallow corn and sugar beet fields to a duck club that my father had joined years earlier when we still lived in Colorado. It wasn't much: a run-down old farm-house set by a sizeable reservoir. But there were usually plenty of ducks about, my father assured me.

By the time we arrived, my father's friend Hank from Denver had already arrived along with his son, Hank Jr. and some people from Kansas we didn't know. I liked Hank Sr., whom we called "Big Hank." He was a gregarious former fighter pilot who'd won a slew of medals in the Pacific during the war. When they fished or hunted together, he and my father were always trying to one-up each other, arguing over who was the better wing shot or which one of them had caught the bigger fish. "I taught your father everything he knows about hunting and fishing," Big Hank would confide in me with a wink. He and Pappy had grown up together in Denver, and, when-ever Big Hank had a couple of drinks, he'd tell me about all the hell he and my father had raised when they were my age and a little older.

Little Hank was a different story altogether. He was a few years older than I, a city kid who thought he was a hot shit. The previous fall he'd gone off to boarding school in the East, but had returned mysteriously before the first term was up. The rumor in Denver was that he'd gotten booted for cheating on an exam.

After dinner he and I did the dishes while our fathers played poker with the men from Kansas, their cigar smoke filling the house. "No one's supposed to know this," Hank Jr. confided in me as we fin-ished drying. "But last year this kid from Colorado Springs was upstairs cleaning his shotgun on one of the bunk beds. The gun went off by accident, and he blew off his brother's arm in the upper bunk."

I wasn't sure if Hank Jr. was making this up to scare me, but I declined his invitation to go upstairs to see if we could find any evidence of the gruesome accident. That night I slept on one of the old sofas downstairs with Big Hank's yellow Lab.

We were in the blind before dawn, the two Hanks, Pappy, and I. It was a cold, clear day. Big Hank noticed I was shivering, and poured me some coffee from the thermos. "All right if Murph has a little of this?" he asked Pappy.

My old man shrugged. "Why not? It might help calm his nerves."

The coffee was laced with brandy. I knew the smell of it from my father's bar. One swallow and my metabolism went into high gear. Two and I felt a pleasant buzzing in my head. Suddenly, I no longer noticed the cold.

Pappy checked out the pump action 20 gauge he'd given me to use, as the sun came up over the corn fields to the east. In the distance I heard the quick "pop, pop" of another hunter's shotgun. "You're up first, Murph, being the youngest," Hank Sr. told me.

I was determined to make up for the debacle on the North Platte. Appealing perhaps to what he perceived as my artistic nature, Pappy had told me that the secret to bird hunting was to think of my shotgun as a paintbrush and "paint over" the bird in one smooth motion as it flew by. This was a much easier notion for me to grasp than the big hand on the clock theory of fly fishing.

The first ducks of the morning came in high and to the gray north. I painted over the lead mallard but missed, as did Hank Jr. "Don't waste any more shells," Pappy advised us. "They're just about out of range."

Soon after, my father and Big Hank nailed three birds in quick succession, the two men arguing good-naturedly over who had killed the third duck. When they left the blind to retrieve the birds and take a piss, Hank Jr. handed me the thermos with a lewd grin, and I eagerly refilled my cup. Maybe he wasn't such a bad kid after all.

For the half hour or so that we sat around the blind waiting for more ducks to come in, both Pappy and Hank Jr. complained how the duck traffic was unusually light that morning. But I didn't mind. I was having a fine time drinking my coffee and letting the first rays of morning sunlight warm my body.

Abruptly Pappy grabbed my shoulder. "Get ready, Murph," he told me. A single mallard was flying in low from the east. His flight path took him directly over the blind.

"Now!" Pappy whispered urgently when the mallard was no more than fifty yards away and coming in fast. I stood up, shotgun at the ready, but was suddenly so dizzy I thought I'd pass out. What had happened to my mallard? I'd momentarily lost it in the sun.

I shot—aimed at where the duck should have been instead of painting over it as Pappy had instructed—and knew at once I'd missed. A second shot and Hank Jr. let out a cry of exaltation. He'd gotten my duck. Pappy shook me violently by the collar of my jacket. "Christ almighty, a blind man could have hit that duck," he said angrily.

Hank Jr. was wearing a big shit-eating grin. I would have liked to use some of my father's self-defense techniques on him, maybe pop him one in the Adam's apple and watch him roll around on the floor of the blind gasping for breath.

"The sun was in the boy's eyes," Hank Sr. offered kindly. He seemed genuinely sorry that it was Hank Jr. and not I who'd downed the mallard.

By now Pappy had let go of my jacket and was looking at me strangely. He must have gotten a whiff of my breath. "Sun, hell," he said disgustedly. "The little bastard is stinking drunk."

From then on Pappy and I rarely hunted together. Clearly he realized that I was nervous around him, and he asked some of his friends to take me out, explaining that the two of us brought out the worst in each other. Away from my father, my buck fever seemed to abate. I still got the jitters, but at least I didn't make a total fool of myself. Hunting with Deb Gast, a neighboring rancher who was one of my parents' close friends, I shot my first antelope out on Wyoming's Red Desert. She and I stalked the skittish herd for hours, crawling on our bellies through the sage like Cheyenne warriors until we were within several hundred yards of our quarry. They bolted when I missed my first shot, but as the antelope raced across the horizon, I downed a little buck with a perfect heart shot. The fact that I'd been aiming at another, larger buck some ten or fifteen yards ahead of him was a secret I wisely kept to myself.

Deb dropped me back at the ranch the following day with the antelope in the back of her pickup truck. "Look what Murph got," she announced proudly when Pappy, Dillon, and my mother came out to greet us. "He dressed it himself."

Pappy clapped me on the back, even embraced me in a rare show of affection. For a brief moment I was the son he'd always wanted, but later that fall when he asked me to go deer hunting with him and Don Edmunds, our foreman, I declined the invitation, opting to visit my grandmother in Denver instead.

By then I'd had my fill of blood sports, and I suppose in some obscure way I wanted to hurt my old man, make him pay for not being one of those fathers I'd read about in the magazines.

AN ARC OF GENERATIONS

by Donald Hall

My father and I used to play catch when he came home tired from the office, in the half hour my mother spent putting dinner on the table. Like so much else between fathers and sons, playing catch was tender and tense at the same time. If he wanted me to be good at baseball for my own sake, he also seemed to *demand* that I be good. I threw the ball into his catcher's mitt. *Atta boy. Put her right there.* I threw straight. But when I tried to put something on it, it flew twenty feet over his head; or it banged into the sidewalk in front of him, breaking stitches and ricocheting into the gutter of Greenway Street; or it went wide to his right and lost itself in Mrs. Davis's bushes; or wide to his left and rolled across the street while drivers swerved their cars.

I was wild. I was *wild*. I had to be wild for my father. What else could I be? Would you have expected me to have *control?*

But I was, myself, the control on him. He had wanted to teach school, to coach and teach history at Cushing Academy in Ashburnham, Massachusetts, as he had done for two years before he married. The salary was minuscule and in the twenties people didn't get married until they had an income to live on. Since he wanted to marry my mother, he made the only decision he could make: He quit

Cushing and went into the family business, and he hated business, and he wept when he fired people, and he wept when he was criticized, and his head shook at night, and he coughed from all the cigarettes, and he couldn't sleep, and he almost died when an ulcer hemorrhaged at forty-two, and ten years later, at fifty-two, he died of lung cancer.

The scene I remember best happened when he was twenty-five and I was almost one year old. So I do not *remember* it at all, but it rolls itself before my eyes with the intensity of a lost memory suddenly found again, more intense than memory can itself ever be, a scene I have fabricated out of pieces of story.

It is 1929, July, a hot Saturday afternoon. At the ballpark near East Rock, in New Haven, Connecticut, just over the Hamden line, my father is playing semipro baseball. I don't know the names of the teams. My mother has brought me in a basket. She sits under an elm tree, in the shade, and lets me crawl when I wake up.

My father is very young and very skinny. When he takes off his cap—the uniform is gray, the bill of the cap blue—his fine hair is parted in the middle. His face is smooth; although he is twenty-five, he could pass for twenty. He plays shortstop, and he is paid twenty-five dollars a game. I don't know where the money comes from. Do they pass the hat? They would never raise so much money. Do they charge admission? They must charge admission, or I am wrong that it was semipro and that he was paid. Or the whole thing is wrong, the story entirely invented. But of course the reality of 1929— my mother and the basket and the shade and the heat—does not matter, not to the memory of the living nor to the bones of the dead, nor even to the fragmentary images of broken light from that day which wander light-years away in unrecoverable space. What matters is my clear and fine knowledge of this day as it happens now, permanently and repeatedly, on a deep layer of the personal Troy.

There, where this Saturday afternoon in 1929 rehearses itself, my slim father performs brilliantly at shortstop. He dives for a low line drive and catches it backhand, somersaults, and stands up displaying the ball. Sprinting into left field with his back to the plate, he catches a fly that almost drops for a Texas leaguer. He knocks down a ground ball, deep in the hole and nearly to third base, picks it up, and throws the man out at first with a peg as flat as the tape a runner breaks. When he comes up to bat, he feels lucky. The opposing pitcher is a side-armer; he always hits side-armers. So he hits two doubles and a triple, drives in two runs and scores two, and his team wins 4 to 3. After the game a man approaches him—while he stands, sweating and tired, with my mother and me in the shade of the elm at the side of the field. The man is a baseball scout. He offers my father a contract to play baseball with the Baltimore Orioles, at that time a minor league team. My father is grateful and flattered; he is proud to be offered the job, but he must refuse. After all, he has just started working at the dairy for his father. It wouldn't be possible to leave the job that he decided so painfully to take. And besides, he adds, there is the baby.

My father didn't tell me that he turned the job down because of me. All that he told me, or I think he told me: He was playing semipro at twenty-five dollars a game; he had a good day in the field, catching a ball over his shoulder running away from the plate; he had a good day hitting, too, because he could always hit a side-armer. He turned down the Baltimore Orioles' offer because he couldn't leave the dairy then, and besides, he knew that he had just been lucky that day. He wasn't really that good.

But maybe he didn't even tell me that. My mother remembers nothing of this story. Or rather she remembers that he played on a team for the dairy, against other businesses, and that she took me to games when I was a baby. But she remembers nothing of semipro, of the afternoon with the side-armer, of the offered contract. Did I make it up? Did my father exaggerate? Men show off, telling stories to their sons.

I don't care.

Baseball is fathers and sons. Football is brothers beating each other up in the backyard, violent and superficial. Baseball is the generations, looping backward forever with a million apparitions of sticks and balls, cricket and rounders, and the games the Iroquois played in Connecticut before the English came. Baseball is fathers and sons playing catch, lazy and murderous, wild and controlled, the profound archaic song of birth, growth, age, and death. This diamond encloses what we are.

FINDING FATHER

by Nick Lyons

My father died three months before I was born, more than half a century ago. On a raw, wet March night, my mother sent him out for some silly knickknack and, four days later, he was dead of pneumonia. All that spring my mother—in love, bereft, numb with guilt—was in shock, so her relatives, to protect her, destroyed all evidence that Nat Ress had ever lived and never again mentioned the man. No one thought Mama would survive, or that I would, but we did—I was born in June—and I got my father's name, to take his place.

I knew none of this until much later, so when I was ten and a stout red-headed friend in Brooklyn told me with absolute authority that, since my mother was not married when I was born, I was a bastard (my new stepfather didn't count), I believed him. There were no photographs of my father, no letters from him to my mother, no private or business papers, no death certificate, no papers relating to their marriage. I know: I scoured the house when everyone was out, hunting in every obscure corner. I found nothing. Whatever the well-meaning relatives missed, my mother must have chucked out, perhaps when she remarried, because my stepfather discouraged any talk about my father, perhaps because he didn't want my half sister to know my mother had been married before. Our family was lousy with secrets.

The closest I came to finding my father was on a June day after I'd

61

returned from the army. I was using my full legal name on my checks then, "Nathan Ress," along with my stepfather's name, "Lyons," though I had always been called "Nicki" and eventually became simply "Nick." I had just given my friend Schmulke Bernstein a check for twenty dollars to repay a debt. He called me about noon. Where had I gotten my name, he asked—the first two parts of it? I told him, and he said he had endorsed the check to his father and his father had said that his best friend, a quarter of a century earlier, had been a man named Nat Ress.

I galloped the thirty-five blocks down Avenue J and, sweating and out of breath, rang Schmulke's doorbell for a full thirty seconds. His father, a mild man who always wore open-backed slippers, and shuffled rather than walked, was quite unprepared for the hour-long grilling I gave him. And all I ever got was that Nat Ress was his "best friend," they "went everywhere together," he was "a terrific guy," he was "swell," he "played a great game of handball."

Even in my twenties, and for twenty-five years after that, I hungered for the authority and wisdom, the yardstick against which to measure myself, the figure against whom to rebel, the man to laugh with or to hate, the model of a million things a father can be. My stepfather was too quietly cruel to love, too bland and safe to hate properly; and then he vanished, too, summarily divorcing my mother, abandoning us all, and starting a new life, full of more secrets.

For years I sought out older friends, mentors in graduate school who became fathers, friends in their sixties who became fathers, bosses, and local elder statesmen. The search for a father is a search for authority outside of yourself; you feel wraithlike, incomplete without him, in whatever form he takes. Too much "father," as Kafka knew, makes the will go mush—too little and the longing can be monstrous. In those years from four to eight, when I was in a boarding school in Peekskill composed mostly of orphans or children from broken families, the longing was worse than monstrous. Inevitably, since they are not you, all fathers—surrogate and real—disappoint.

When my mother died a couple of years ago, I learned there was a family plot somewhere in Queens and when we got to it on that cold March day, I stood with my four grown kids around me—to whom I've been who knows what stripe of a father, pouring out to them a pent-up volcano of love, but *there*—and my wife of a quarter of a century, with our arms around each other, and tossed some roses down after Rose, who hadn't had such a good time of it here.

When the last few words had been said, I looked across the gray sea of stones, the silent acres and acres of minor monuments, and then at the stones near the raw hole beside which we stood. It was raining and the exposed soil had turned to mud. Then I turned my head slightly, to the stone to the left of where my mother's would go, and there, with some dates, the last one in March 1932, was my first name, "Nathan Ress."

It was just an old stone, with some dates and a name; it wasn't much and I'm not sure why—since it was time, in my fifties, with a name of my own, to stop searching anyway—but I've never since looked for a father.

AFTER MY STEPFATHER'S DEATH

by Wesley McNair

Again it is the moment before I left home
for good, and my mother is sitting quietly
in the front seat while my stepfather pulls me
and my suitcase out of the car and begins
hurling my clothes, though now
I notice for the first time how the wind
unfolds my white shirt and puts its slow
arm in the sleeve of my blue shirt and lifts them
all into the air above our heads so beautifully
I want to shout at him to stop and look up
at what he has made, but of course when I turn
to him, a small man, bitter even this young
that the world will not go his way, my stepfather
still moves in his terrible anger, closing the trunk,
and closing himself into the car as hard as he can,
and speeding away into the last years of his life.

THE RAFT

by David Ewing Duncan

I

Sammy Wells kicked at something in the weeds. I thought king-snake, *Lampropeltis getulus*, and went into a snaker's crouch, forked stick raised like a harpoon, cloth bag ready. The bag twitched. Rat snake, *Elaphe obsoleta*. Later, my dad measured it: two feet, seven inches.

"Loosen up, man," said Sammy. "It's no snake." He kicked again with the toe of his Red Ball Jets sneakers, trying to work loose the mat of dead bluestem. "It's a piece of wood or somethin'."

We dropped to our knees and tore at the weeds with pudgy boys' hands until we reached a gray slab of wood about the size of a door, with rusted oarlocks on either side.

It wasn't much of a boat. Whoever built it started with a thick piece of plywood and added two homemade seat backs, oarlocks, a storage box, and inflatable rubber tubes stapled to the underside.

Sammy had his theory. A year earlier, two serial killers, Ed "Jinx" Jeevey and Billy Rodríguez, escaped from the federal peniten-tiary twenty-five miles up the Kaw River. The police grabbed them near our lake, in old man Dixon's barn. Dixon pumped gas at the Skelly station. He always had a cigarette stuck to his lower lip. When he growled at us boys to stay away from the station, the cig flapped up and down, the smoke doing zigzags. If not for TV, no one would've believed old man Dixon found the killers sleeping behind his hogs.

Sammy said the killers must've escaped in the raft, paddling down the Kaw and up the spillway into our lake. "They dragged it up here," said Sammy, "and hid it in the weeds." The idea that the killers had to haul the raft two miles uphill made Jinx and Rodríguez, two losers still waiting to be electrocuted all these years later, that much more sinister.

We dragged the raft to the ruins of a stone farmhouse in a stand of cottonwoods by Mouse Creek. Boys' secrets littered the ground: condoms, .22 shells, skeletons of one or two small rodents killed for no good reason, rain-drenched *Playboys*, minus the nudes. In November, we had the old house to ourselves, though the older boys might come back anytime. "We gotta cover it up good," said Sammy, ripping dead branches off trees. I scooped up dead leaves.

After hiding the boat, we swore the usual pact of secrecy, though that never stopped me from telling my dad just about everything. I was at an uncertain age, eleven or twelve. I could stop and figure it out exactly, but what's the point? I must've been in sixth grade, an age when a boy first has secrets worth keeping to himself.

I ran home fast along trails and overgrown four-wheeler tracks until I reached the Grissoms' house at the edge of the trees. My house was five down from the trees. I was panting when I took a sharp turn into our driveway. My face was flush, hot against cool November air.

"What's the big rush?" asked Dad, looking up from a shovelful of decorative rocks, each the size of a walnut. His face was smeared with dirt like a boy's, his beard unshaven over the weekend. Dad loved digging, cutting, toting, to be master of his two acres. This was his final project of the year, spreading rocks in a bed between the kitchen deck and the lawn. He had draped heavy black plastic over blue-gray clay to keep out weeds. Four circular wire cages protected cherry saplings shipped from Japan. Because his work kept him away so much, he was late planting them. Later that winter, two died.

I started to tell Dad about the raft, but something stopped me. It wasn't so much the pact with Sammy, but a sudden realization that

Dad knew nothing about our discovery. The raft was *mine*, my project, something apart from my parents. I held up my snake bag. *"Elaphe obsoleta,"* I said. "Least I think so."

"Let's measure it," he said. "Then you can give me a hand with these rocks."

"Josh has a secret," Dad whispered to Mom as the weeks went by, winking in my direction. He let me use his tools, saying he wasn't going to ask why I needed them. "Just be careful with sharp edges," he said.

"Come on, Dad," I said, annoyed at being treated like a child.

"You must have told him, man," Sammy said at the old stone house. "Why else would he give you all these friggin' tools?"

"I stole 'em," I said, feeling my color rise at the lie.

"All *right*," said Sammy.

Sammy Wells was a borderline fat boy. He wore blue jeans marked HEFTY in the boys' section at Macy's, but he could scramble as fast as us skinny kids. His dad was an F-4 fighter pilot killed in 1966. Sammy said he took out four "gook" MIGs before his engines exploded. Sammy was cold. With his Crayolas he drew the F-4 breaking up, bits of flesh and flaming metal, a bloody arm and shoulder dripping with blood, the pocket stenciled with WELLS.

In third or fourth grade, he brought his dad's medals to show-and-tell, clusters, stars, ribbons, and the flag they draped over Captain Wells's coffin. When I asked Dad about his medals, he rummaged in his sock drawer. He found two short rows of service bars and a single dangling star, awarded when a distant North Korean cruiser took a potshot at his cargo frigate. At the time, I felt bitterly disappointed.

Later, in high school, Sammy became a true fat boy, moody, unwashed, dangerous in a vague way, like he might go berserk anytime. When I was a junior, he stopped me in the hall between classes to announce that his dad really had been a sergeant, a mechanic who repaired airplane engines in Vietnam. He drowned after getting drunk at a party in Da Nang. "The medals," said Sammy, "came from a flea market." Sammy Wells and I hadn't been close for years, so this abrupt admission struck me as bizarre. Sammy smelled of cannabis. His eyes were glassy, red-rimmed. He spooked around with the Dungeons and Dragons crowd, quoting Black Sabbath lyrics about suicide. I thought about my dad and his single little star, forgotten in a drawer of socks.

II

Days, sometimes weeks passed when it was too cold to work on the raft. In December, during a warm spell, Sammy painted FUGITIVE on its bow in black letters, after the serial killers. "I'll be Jinx," he said. "You be Rodríguez."

"Those guys slashed people's throats. Cut off their nuts and stuff."

"That's *righhhhhhht!!*" Sammy screamed, coming at me with epoxy on the end of a stick. He was patching the tubes under our ship. "I'm going to epoxy your nuts to your forehead, Rodríguez," he shouted. I went for his feet, tackled him, and told him to stop calling me Rodríguez.

"Okay, okay," he laughed, leaves flying as I tried to pin him down, *"Rodríguez."*

In January, after an ice storm, the tools I hid with the raft disappeared. Dad's hammer, two wrenches, screwdrivers. "I'm a dead man," I said, standing by a fire Sammy had blazing against the stone house.

"I thought you *stole* 'em," he taunted.

"Screw off," I said, trying to think of what to tell Dad.

I told him nothing. His winking had stopped. I wasn't seeing him much. He seemed to have forgotten about my "secret," preoccupied more than ever with his job.

It was a strange time for Dad and me. Maybe winter depressed him because he couldn't work outside. Maybe this was the beginning of the trouble between him and Mom that never quite led to a divorce, but turned them into strangers by the time I left for college. When

Dad came home from work, usually long after dinner, he sat in the living room with a beer, his eyes closed, listening to the same Miles Davis album over and over. (I still think of him sitting there when I hear *Kind of Blue*.) Sometimes, he'd get testy about school-work unfinished or dishes left out. Otherwise, we hardly spoke to each other.

One night he called me into the living room. I was ready for bed, in my pajamas. The room was dim, a yellowish color, lit by a single lamp across the room from where Dad sat with a highball. "Son," he said wearily, "you didn't finish the driveway. You *know* it gets harder to shovel when we drive the cars over the snow." He rubbed his brow and looked up. "What am I going to do with you?"

"Dad," I said, "it's a really long driveway. I remember when you used to help me."

He looked up. I was surprised to see a flash of anger, quickly checked. "Josh," he said, "I need your help. My work, as you know, is not going well. This oil embargo is killing us. I can't pay for gas to keep the trucks going. And building materials . . ." He trailed off. "I want to help you with the driveway, but I'm just too tired right now."

This was the winter my father's architecture business failed, when he was struggling to pay debts and maintain a thirty-year-old business founded by his father, though I didn't realize this at the time. The office was an integral part of my father, a symbol of his individuality. He would go on to join a larger firm and make his name over again as a company man, but that wasn't what he wanted. "You know I miss doing things outside," he said, almost whispering.

"It's a long driveway," I said tentatively.

"Josh, it's up to you to take over for me while I'm trying to straighten out this mess at the office."

"Maybe you could help me before work tomorrow," I said with a smile, expecting him to say, "Okay, Josh, just you and me." Instead, his face went taut.

"Didn't you *hear* what I said? I don't have time! I have to work every hour of every day to make enough money for you and the family. Do you know where your bike and your toy cars come from?

Money. Who brings home the money?" He glared at me. "I want that driveway shoveled *now.*"

"Now? But I'm in my pajamas!"

"Do it!" he shouted, waving his tall boy in my direction. "I'm tired of hearing excuses."

I pushed the snow, heavy and wet, into precise piles at the edge of the driveway. Two spotlights over the garage lit up the snow. Blackness, a void, extended beyond the lights. Cold penetrated my thin pajama bottoms and a sweatshirt hastily put on. I wanted the cold to hurt. I wanted something awful to happen to me, to get back at my father. My breath came out in quick, white clouds, more from anger than exertion. Sweat on my head turned icy at the edge of my stocking cap.

Every minute, every push of the shovel, I expected my dad to come out and apologize, to make a fuss over the cold, to gently chastise me for not bundling up properly. My skin grew numb, but Dad didn't come.

My muscles ached and the void beyond the lights grew deeper. I thought about the raft. "I gotta get out of here," I thought darkly. "I'll get Sammy and we'll paddle to the Kaw and right out of here."

I shoveled on toward the void, no longer noticing the cold, planning my escape. When the lake thawed, I'd make them come after me.

I started spending more time at Sammy Wells's house, down the street. Mrs. Wells smoked constantly and never cleaned up the house. I still think of Sammy's kitchen when I smell sour milk. They left it out for a cat named Billy, who disappeared for days, leaving his milk to rot. It was a house where I always seemed to be tripping over old, half-filled cups of coffee, and no one cared.

We built a city for our Matchbox cars on the Wellses' living room floor, playing there every day after school until Mrs. Wells had an argument with Max, her boyfriend.

"You fucking bitch!" he screamed at her. I was stunned to hear grown-ups talking like that, but Sammy kept on playing. "I'm taking the money away *now*."

"Take your goddamned money," she screeched, slinging a dirty plate at the boyfriend. It struck his forehead with a loud *thunk*, like knuckles on a door.

"Goddamn," said Max, touching his forehead and looking at the blood, "goddamn!"

He was still saying "goddamn" when Sammy Wells grabbed my arm and we took off. We ran down the street and the snowy trails into the dense mist all the way to the old stone house. Inside its wet, ruined walls we caught our breath, standing over the raft.

"I *hate* winter," said Sammy, kicking viciously at a row of icicles, smashing them all.

"We gotta get out of here," I said.

"Like Jinx and Rodríguez," said Sammy.

III

In February, the snow receded to traces under trees and against foundations. The earth was gray, the trees above the old stone house mournful. Sammy and I were hammering a wooden spoiler on the raft when we heard the thin whine of a transistor radio. We had no time to hide.

"Hey now, look at this," said Nick Rhodes, fourteen. He exhaled cigarette smoke, walking with three other eighth-graders. "Is that a boat?"

"It looks like a piece of shit to me," said another boy.

"You think that's gonna float?" said Phil Henderson, who had the longest hair at school and wore pointed black shoes. Later that year, they kicked him out of school for breaking windows in the first-floor boys' room. Everybody said he dropped acid and went wacko.

"Yeah, it's gonna float," said Sammy, standing up.

"You're a ballsy little pussy," said Nick Rhodes.

Phil Henderson took a deep drag off his cigarette and punched Sammy hard on the shoulder. We called it a Monkey Knuckle. Hit the shoulder hard. See if the other kid flinches. Sammy, cool as he was, didn't move.

"This boat'll never float," said Henderson. He punched him again, hard as he could. Sammy took it. "You can trust me."

"I think Henderson was the jerk who stole my dad's tools," I said when they left. We were dragging the raft down a four-wheeler road into a dense thicket where a farm pond used to be. It was our most secret spot in the field, where we hid during the summer, when the older boys hung out at the old stone house. Sammy once hid two cigarettes in a hollow tree inside the thicket. But they got soggy before he got up the nerve to smoke them.

"Henderson's a prick," said Sammy.

"Do you think he'd mess with the boat?"

"He will," said Sammy, "if he can find it."

A thick fog hung over the field the next time we heard the whiny transistor radio, off in the distance. "Quick," I said to Sammy, "get rid of that fire." He threw wet leaves on the flames. "Crap, they're gonna smell the smoke."

"Shut up," whispered Sammy. "I think they're just goin' to the old house to smoke."

Someone turned off the transistor radio.

"All we got to do," shouted Phil Henderson through the trees, "is follow the smoke, and I bet we'll find a couple of pussies with a boat." Sammy and I crouched low behind the hollow tree. "It ain't *never* gonna float," Henderson yelled. "Not *never.*"

Sammy stood up to say something, but I held him down.

Phil Henderson, whom I just wanted to avoid, suddenly loomed large in my life. On the bus, he would grin ominously from his seat in the back. I think he wanted to get at Sammy through me. Sammy had passed his test of cool, or pain, or whatever. Sammy also was getting big. That winter he grew at least four inches. Just like that, his voice turned low and gravelly, while mine remained high. His muscles rounded out. Mine stayed lean. Henderson, of course, probably went through puberty at birth. He was a head taller than me and could grow a thin mustache. "How's your little boat project?" he would whisper while passing me in the hallway at school.

I wanted to tell my dad about Phil Henderson, to ask him what to do. But Dad wasn't around. He hovered on the edge of my life and said little unless I got in the way.

In March, Dad asked about his tools. I wanted to tell him they were lost, but I didn't know how he'd react. I lied and told him they were over at Sammy's.

"What am I gonna do?" I asked Sammy, up at the boat. He was smoking a cigarette, sitting in one of the raft's two plywood seats.

"There's only one thing we can do," said Sammy. "Steal some new ones. Like I stole these cigarettes."

"You did?"

"Yeah. From my mom's new boyfriend. He's a dumbass. He leaves half-finished packs all over the house and forgets 'em. Last night, I took a couple." He handed me one, and a pack of matches. I hesitated. "Come on," he said, "don't be a pussy." He lit a cigarette for me. "Jesus, Harper, just try it."

"I don't want to, man."

"Wussy," said Sammy. He leaped up, grabbed me around the neck, and tried to force the cigarette between my lips. "Take a puff, man."

I squirmed, unable to believe that Sammy Wells could hold me that long. He had grown that much bigger. I finally shook him loose. "Asshole," I said.

"Come on, *Joshy*," he said, "or should I say *Rodríguez?*"

I brought the cig to my lips, sucked, and felt a sharp sting in my throat. When I coughed, Sammy told me to try again. "Close up your throat, man. Don't inhale. Do it like this." He sucked a tiny drab of smoke and blew it out. I did the same, and managed to hold back the cough.

"I can't steal the tools, Sammy," I told him, holding the cig between my fingers. "My dad would know."

"So, we rip 'em off and you tell your old man you lost 'em and you've been saving up your allowance to replace 'em."

"Sammy, how much allowance do you think I get?"

IV

In early March, the temperature jumped up into the fifties, and the lake thawed. High winds broke the ice into great sheets. Angry, white-capped waves smashed the sheets into splinters.

"It's time," said Sammy on the telephone.

For weeks, Sammy and I had been gathering supplies. A little here, a little there, so nobody would notice. Bread. Peanut butter. Cokes. Chips. When the warm weather came, we took extra clothes and some of Dad's camping gear. Sammy brought firecrackers, two record albums, his father's medals. Thinking back, I realize Sammy really meant to run away, while I was just trying to make a point.

We had no idea where we were going. Sammy and I planned to haul the raft to the wooded end of the lake, where no one would see us, and head for the spillway. There we'd carry *Fugitive* around the dam into the wide creek leading from the lake to the Kaw.

That Saturday, Sammy and I got up at dawn. Working in silence under a clear sky, we packed up and began dragging the raft. *Fugitive* rested on a wooden trolley we made with eight wagon wheels. Sammy found the wheels in the junkyard down by the Kaw, near the sand plant. He pulled the front with a thick rope. I pushed from behind.

The arrangement worked fine for about a half hour, until we came to an uphill.

"Come on, Wells, are you *pulling*?" I shouted, my head dripping in the warm weather.

"Are you *pushing*?"

"It's gonna take us years to get to the lake," I said.

"We gotta couple more of these little hills," he said, "then it's downhill all the way."

"Hey Sammy," I said, straining up the next uphill, "did you hear something?"

"What?" said Sammy.

"Shhhh." I strained to listen through the warm, damp silence of the trees. "I thought I heard a radio," I whispered.

"I don't hear anything," said Sammy, who had tied an orange bandana around his head. "Let's get this stupid thing down to the lake before I croak."

"What if they're out there?"

"Don't be a wuss, man."

We passed close to my street about midmorning. I could see the Grissoms' house through the trees, and the top of a hickory in my yard. It would be hours before my parents would miss me. This made me feel good, that I knew and they didn't.

Below the Grissoms', a steep hill sloped down to the lake. *Fugitive* rolled easily down a wide trail, though the loud rattling of the wheels made us nervous. It seemed like the whole lake could hear the *ratatatata*.

"Hold on!" I shouted, "not so fast!"

At the bottom, we had to cross Lake Shore Drive. Traffic was light, but steady, with a car coming every few minutes. It wouldn't have mattered if anyone saw us, two boys dragging what looked like a door with seats. But Sammy and I were primed for intrigue. What if a neighbor saw us? What if one of our parents drove past?

We lay on our stomachs in the wet weeds off the road, *Fugitive* beached above us in the trees. The cold wetness of weeds and soil, smelling like rotten leaves, soaked through my sweatshirt and jeans. I shivered, waiting.

Then it was quiet for several minutes, with only one car driving past. It was Sue Wilson's mother. Rumor had it Sue Wilson would show her breasts, such as they were, for a dollar in the boys' room. Mrs. Wilson was one of the faceless parents who came and went at Lake Cibola, buying gas and a carton of milk at the Skelly, driving kids to swim meets, smoking cigarettes.

Sammy and I dashed across the street, toting the raft with what seemed to us superhuman strength, darting into the strip of trees between the lake and the road. We ran into the trees, laughing, exhilarated. The lake glimmered through the trees, a blue sheet in the sun, ice clinging to the shore like white glass. Then we heard something that stopped us cold.

"Damn that radio," Sammy whispered.

"Why can't they leave us alone?"

"Maybe they're just up on the road. Maybe they don't know we're here."

We crouched low as the radio got louder, then trailed off.

"Let's get this thing into the water," said Sammy. "Those assholes may be back."

We had planned to take *Fugitive* to a small, abandoned pier in the southern swamp, but that was an hour away. "Let's put in here," I said.

Silently, we stowed food in the strongbox, tied down sleeping bags and the big canvas tent with twine, inserted oars into oarlocks. The bank was steep, a wall of mud and roots three feet high. We lifted the raft off the trolley and tied a thick rope onto *Fugitive's* bow. Using a small maple as a hoist, Sammy belayed the line while I pushed her over the lip.

"Hold it," I shouted as the boat lurched from horizontal to vertical. I dug my heels into the mud and held tight to keep the raft from falling too fast. "Let it out slowly!"

"This bitch is heavy," said Sammy.

The bow dropped, inch by inch, until it crashed through the brittle shelf of ice clinging to the mud above the water. Then *Fugitive*, its pontoons lathered in mud, slid into the water. After bobbing for a moment, she stabilized, the deck floating a good half foot above the water.

"She's in!" I shouted.

V

Lake Cibola was three hundred fifty acres of muddy creekwater held back by a clay dam a mile long. In the early-afternoon sun it looked deep blue, almost black. High, white clouds were rising over the western ridge. Rain was coming, but that didn't matter. We sat like princes on our plywood thrones, still holding on to the shore, arranging our oars and testing the balance of the boat, when a boulder suddenly hit the water with a splash as tall as a man. Frigid droplets rained down and *Fugitive* lurched.

"Holy shit," said Sammy.

"Get 'em!" shouted the unmistakable voice of Nick Rhodes.

"Push us off!" I said, starting to paddle furiously.

"Fire two!" Another basketball-sized rock hit the water, this time several feet away.

"Get it closer!" That was Phil Henderson's voice. "Drop 'em right next to the boat. Get 'em wet!"

"Flip 'em," said someone else.

Sammy and I tried desperately to paddle, to get away, to swing our oars together like we'd practiced on dry land, but it was hopeless. Our strokes were out of synch, too strong and then too soft. We spun in jerky quarter circles, stirring up a froth of water and mud and getting nowhere.

"Look at the pussies," laughed Henderson as another boulder fell. This time it grazed the stern, breaking off a small piece of plywood.

"Hey, somebody's gonna get hurt," I yelled, my anger at their stupidity overcoming my fear. "Those rocks could break open someone's head."

"That's right," said Henderson. "Yours! Fire four!" Another hit, this time square on the stern. The force of the rock punched a small hole in the deck. *Fugitive* lunged, nearly knocking us off.

"Josh," said Sammy, "give me your lighter."

"What?"

"Give me the friggin' lighter," he whispered frantically. "I got cherry bombs!"

I fumbled in my pocket and handed it over. He lit the fuse and tossed the firecracker up the embankment. The bomb exploded with the force of a quarter stick of dynamite. Sammy grinned. I said, "All *right*!"

"What the hell was that?" shouted Rhodes.

"Little bastards got cherries!"

Sammy pitched a second bomb and said, "Let's get the f-u-c-k out of here."

"Unclamp your oar," I said, "it'll be easier if we paddle like a canoe."

"You paddle, man, and I'll pitch bombs."

I freed my oar and crawled unsteadily to the bow, kneeled, and started paddling. I knew we only had to go a couple of yards to hit the current where Mouse Creek ran into the lake. Then we'd be out of range.

Sammy was a wild man, tossing cherries, M-80s, and strings of Black Cats up the hill. A cloud of blue smoke rose off the bank. The older boys cursed. They lobbed another boulder, but missed by ten feet. They tossed smaller rocks and half-smoked cigarettes, which also missed.

"That thing still ain't gonna float," shouted Henderson. By then, we were fifteen feet offshore and hitting the steady current that was fed by melting snow. The boys onshore kept tossing stones. Some of them hit, but we were too far away for it to matter.

"It ain't gonna float for long," Henderson yelled. "You can count on that."

"What did he mean by that?" I asked Sammy, paddling in the stern.

"Any of those assholes got a boat?" asked Sammy.

"Rhodes's old man does. Their dock's on the east side of the lake. But it's probably out of water this time of year."

"Let's hope it is, man."

The current took us out into a large, wooded cove on Cibola's south end. The air was still and clear, the sun warm on our faces. We kept paddling, staying well off the shore, in case Henderson reappeared with more rocks. We decided that Rhodes's boat *had* to be out of the water. Anyway, I said, he had to get gas, get the keys from his old man, and on and on.

"We're home free," Sammy said.

VI

In Kansas, March weather can be fickle. As we paddled, the cloud over the western ridge blew in our direction, driven by a powerful prairie windstorm.

"Crap, man, it's gonna rain," said Sammy.

"If we paddle our butts off," I said, "we can make the spillway and set up the tent by the river."

But the clouds were moving fast. Before we knew it, they rolled across the lake, low and foggy, obliterating the sun, then the shore. Before we could do anything a cold and clammy mist engulfed the raft.

Raindrops began to fall as we paddled toward shore. I took deep strokes, pulling, straining. It was hard going against the current.

"Josh, hold on," said Sammy. "Are we even moving? Josh! Stop, man. Look."

I stopped and watched the water. Sammy was right. The current was carrying us backward, out into the lake.

"That's weird," I said, "we were doing fine before." I took another couple of strokes. "Sammy, does the boat seem to be dragging?"

"Whataya mean?"

"Like the pontoons are losin' air? Look. The deck's droppin'."

"We're losing air, man."

"Henderson," I said.

"He *said* this thing wasn't gonna float for long."

"It could've been your lousy patch job."

"Screw you, man," said Sammy. "We tested it. They must've poked holes in the tubes. They do that with teachers' cars at school. Use little pins. It takes hours before the tires go flat. That way you don't get caught."

"Sammy, let's paddle." I plunged my paddle into the mass of gray water as the rain started to fall in heavy sheets. "Paddle!" I shouted over the rain. Sammy started working.

The cold rain soaked my head and clothes, but I kept paddling: *plunge, pull; plunge, pull.* I couldn't see anything in the dense grayness. Where was the shore?

"Josh, man, it's not working," Sammy shouted over the roaring storm. "The *Fugitive* is sinking, man. We aren't gonna make it!"

"Keep paddling," I said. The deck was definitely dropping, faster now. It was just a couple of inches above the water. Waves were breaking over the deck. "Sammy, you gotta keep paddling! I know we're almost there!"

"Ah, hell," he said, "we aren't gonna make it, Josh."

The storm raged on when I heard a new sound, a high-pitched roar. An engine!

"Do you hear that?" said Sammy. "Is it Henderson?"

I waited for the boat to break into sight through the fog. The roar, however, came close and then started to move away. Then it cut out, as if someone was stopping. The raft was really sinking now. The water was an inch below the deck.

"Hey! Over here!" I screamed. I didn't care if it *was* Henderson. "Over here!"

But the voice shouting my name did not belong to Phil Henderson. It was loud, shouted over a bullhorn. "Joshua! Joshua Harper!" It was my father.

He lifted us off the raft and into our boat like we were dolls. He said nothing, but gave us each a blanket under the boat's awning, where it was mostly dry. "I'm sorry," I said to Dad, wanting to cry, but unable to force the tears.

VII

The squall ended before we got back to our dock. Just like that, the sun came out, low over the western ridge. My dad tied up the boat. He said nothing during the trip back, except to tell us that one of the older boys had called to tell him we might be in trouble. He thought it was Nick Rhodes, but the boy wouldn't give his name.

"Sammy," said my dad, as he secured the boat, "go to my car and wait."

I stood still, freezing in my blanket. I felt small as Dad loomed over me, his hair soaked, his beard unshaven on a Saturday afternoon.

"Josh, give me your hand," he said, his voice dark and angry.

I didn't understand.

"Your hand!" he shouted. I held it out, trying to keep it from shaking. He took it in his large palm. "Come here," he said, giving me a rough pull. I staggered in his grip to the edge of the dock. The water below was black and cold. "Put your hand in the water," he said.

"What?"

"In the water!"

He pulled me down to my knees and thrust my hand into the lake, holding it down by the wrist. I wriggled, unable to break his grip.

"Does it hurt?" he asked. I remained silent, wincing as the cold cut into my hand.

"It does hurt, doesn't it? You know how long you would have lasted in that water? Thirty seconds? Maybe a minute?"

He let go of my hand. I drew it painfully out of the water. It felt strange, looked the color of dried blood. He pointed at a rock on the dock we used to hold things down in the wind. "Pick it up," he said in a low growl. I shook my hand, touching it with my good hand, pushing gently with my finger. The red turned white and then, when I removed my finger, red again. There was no feeling. I wanted to cry out, to scream that my father had killed my hand. But I said nothing.

"Pick up the rock, damn you," he said.

I tried, but my hand was dead. I strained to make the fingers move, to take hold of the rock. I wanted to pick it up and throw it at my father. But he never gave me the chance. Abruptly, he walked up the catwalk, leaving me alone.

Later that spring, Dad's business failed. He and Mom stopped sleeping in the same room. My father must have been on the point of realizing that his life would be one of modest achievements, despite high expectations. Yet none of this mattered as Dad walked up the catwalk that afternoon. He had just saved the life of his son. His strides were powerful. For a few moments nothing could stop him. He was immortal, a product of the wind, the squall, and a fury he probably never felt again.

PROMISES

by Kenneth Barrett

When my father died we both were too young. He was forty-one
and I sixteen, a boy barely on the verge of manhood, when he
pulled the trigger on the shotgun. Now, nearly twenty-five years
later, I am almost the age my father was when, on a hot and humid
morning in August, he ended his life and left behind a wife and four
children.

The evening before my father's death, I had slept at a friend's
house and was not at home to hear the sound of the gun—that
particular horror befell my three younger sisters and mother.
But in my mind's eye I can clearly see my father sitting on
the edge of my bed, the twin barrels staring him in the face,
while downstairs my sisters and mother attend to their household
routines.

I hear the gun's sudden, rude explosion, feel the shattering of the
house's morning rhythm, and see my mother racing up the stairs to
my room, where she finds my father slumped on the bed, gun by his
side, blood draining from his once lovely head.

My mother, who finds coping with even minor illnesses difficult,
is suddenly faced with the violent, incomprehensible death of her
husband. Although she rejects as fact what her eyes see, my mother
screams incoherently at the truth lying before her.

"Ken, you'd better get home right away. There's a problem at
your house," were the words I remember coming from my friend,

his face ashen and voice quivering. I took off running, my breath already made short by fear. As my house came into sight I left the road and cut across the field beside it. In the yard I could see police cars and my sisters standing by the front door, their eyes filled with tears.

"Daddy shot himself," one of them said as I approached.

"Is he dead?" I asked, already knowing the answer.

A few days after his death, it fell to me to take the blood-soaked mattress to the dump. I remember standing in front of a mound of debris with the mattress across my back and shoulders and not wanting to throw it away. How could I? After all, the blood covering it was the same that ran through my own veins. I remember how I dreaded leaving a part of my father so exposed and unprotected—so terribly alone. People I did not know would stare at his spent blood and conjure up images of his last desperate act. The sour, sticky blood that covered the mattress was, I realized, my last physical contact with my father. I wept, my shoulders shuddering in spasms, as I heaved the mattress onto the mound and walked away.

I revisit that scene in my mind nearly every day of my life. I see a boy struggling with the weight and awkwardness of the mattress, with the horror of unexpected death and his sense of duty. It is a scene that fills me with deep sadness and compassion for the boy, who at times seems so distant and detached that he could be someone else. Only he is me, of course, and the sight of him reaching his hand to the back of his neck to touch his father's blood, left there by the mattress, breaks my heart. I see him clearly as he showers and watches through eyes blurred by tears as the blood and water, diluted to the lightest shade of pink, disappear down the drain.

For years I tried to hide the pain that my father's suicide caused me. I pretended the trauma of that morning in August no longer bothered me. But the truth is, the horror and finality of his death were *always* with me, as was the question: Why? Why did my father take his own life? Was it his deep depression, a side effect brought on by the drugs he took for high blood pressure? Or was it the result of growing up with a mother so emotionally crippled that she infected her son with self-hatred?

After the full weight of my father's death hit me, I felt abandoned and alone. I began to question the lessons he had taught me—the validity of his caring and loving. Were these, I wondered, all lies? I could not bear to ask anyone other than myself. And I was without answers.

Like most sons, I had emulated my father since I could remember. Up until his death I wanted nothing in the world so much as to be like him. But to continue in this vein after his death would, it seemed to me, mean certain death. I actually lived with the fear that someday I, too, would commit suicide. And that fear became my father's most enduring legacy to me.

My defense against such a frightening legacy was a promise to myself that I would live to be older than my father was on the day he died. I would prove to myself, my father's ghost, and the world at large that I was stronger and better than he had been. Then I went forward as if on a crusade, armed with a promise that made me determined to survive and become a man.

In the years that followed, when my circle of friends was forever growing and changing, questions about my home and family came up frequently. Inevitably someone would ask about my parents, and I would say that my mother lived in New York but that my father had passed away years ago.

"He must have been young when he died," they almost always said.

"Yes," I would reply, hoping that would be the end of it. As often as not, though, they would persist and ask if my father had died of cancer or in an accident.

When this happened, and I felt obliged to answer, I would be truthful in my reply. From the uncomfortable silence that followed I learned that to die of cancer or a heart attack was tragic but

acceptable, while dying of self-inflicted gunshot was shameful . . .
for both the dead and the living.

For years my father's ghost and my promise to myself remained
hidden while I went to college, married my sweetheart, held good
and interesting jobs, and became a father myself. The exigencies of
daily living were such that only now, over two decades later, am I
beginning to understand how completely that vow to live longer
than my father has influenced my life. Every action I have taken,
every decision I have made, every issue affecting my life, has been
subject to the hidden promise and its ghostly keeper.

It was a chance conversation that brought the ghost out of hiding
and into the light. "My father died when we were both too young," I
said to a friend not long ago. That single utterance was the beginning
of a journey on which I began to revisit the boy who lives inside me,
and, since then, I have come to realize that aspects of my arrogance,
anger, sarcasm, and wit were parts of a lifelong disguise used to mask
the fear my father had bequeathed me.

Now, the fact that I will soon be older than my father was when he
died no longer matters to me, and I will not celebrate or honor that
promise to myself. So repugnant and hurtful is the prospect of con-
tinuing a life filled with such fears that I can now tell the boy inside
me to let go and be free. I can look in the mirror and say to him,
"Give it up, let the ghost go, be free of your promise and begin
healing."

I will never know why my father ended his life, and that fact I'm
learning to accept. I do know, however, and know it well, that
connected as we are, my father and I are not the same: My father
chose death and I choose life; he for his reasons, I for mine. And with
that knowledge I can see my father's life and death in a new light,
one which allows me to feel kindness and gratitude toward that
troubled and unhappy man.

I realize that more than any other person, my father taught me
many of life's most important lessons. I was taught them with love
and patience and compassion, and I know they are the basis for

much of who and what I am today. So subtle were his teachings, though, that I never knew they were his until I became a parent myself and saw my father in me as I began to shape my own children's lives.

Today I have a new promise, one that is not hidden and has nothing to do with death or survival or ghosts. Now I strive to be as careful and gentle with my son as my father was with his. I am trying very hard to be these things because I understand that what I say and do will live with him long beyond my time, just as what my father said and did survived his time. And though I know we are different, I am grateful for what I have of my father in me. It is my gift, my promise to myself and my children.

THREE-DOLLAR DOGS

by William Kittredge

All their doors stood open on that upstairs hallway, so the nurses could hear if someone called out. Those old people had buzzers, buttons they could push, but mostly they forgot and just shouted in their thin voices. You could hear everything. It was an elegant house that had been turned into a home for the aged, and it echoed.

Parade rest.

My grandfather would whisper commands and tell me that he was with Teddy Roosevelt in Cuba. He would play a little wheezing make-believe bugle on his fist, blowing *charge* the way Teddy would have liked it. This was his joke.

Al had never been in the military; I understand now that he was really talking, in some metaphoric way, about his life with my grandmother. But he had seen Teddy Roosevelt give a speech in Butte when he was a young man working the mines.

"Right, left . . . about face." He would be whispering, his lips moving, until he remembered and caught me watching and shook his head. In the silence I could hear the soft footsteps of the nurses on the parquet hardwood floors left over from the days when the house was home to lumber barons.

"The King of France don't live any better," he would say, talking about his life in that room with its high lavender ceiling and cupids circling the overhead light fixture. The windows overlooked summery afternoons in run-down formal gardens. Beyond the

91

stonework back wall of the garden there was a long hayfield slope to the Willamette River where the water sometimes ran purple from the dumpings of the beet cannery upstream. The foothills of the Cascade Mountains rose into the early mists, steep and wooded like the foothills you see in Oriental woodcuts of heaven.

We would get a wheelchair from one of the orderlies, and I would push him along the hard-packed gravel paths between the un-trimmed topiary shrubs (dogs and pigs and horses) and the swelling red and lavender and golden beds of summer flowers. We would head down the driveway and out on the street that looped over to the river. Al liked that, me and him and the wheelchair out there on the street mixing with the traffic.

"We're just fine here," he would say, "fancy as the King of France." He'd look to me then, and shake his head, a quick and almost furtive movement, like there was a loose bone in his ear which had been there all his life, and he couldn't live unless he heard its tiny rattle every so often. Just that sharp, habitual jerk of the head. Sometimes he would pass one of his broken hands over his eyes at the same time, his fingers thick and the calluses softened but still traced with cracks from a lifetime of blacksmithing; a tentative gesture, as if he might be wiping away cobwebs.

The King of France. Or England. Or Russia. I was frightened and embarrassed by the fact that he would be dying soon, because I hadn't seen him much in recent years. Not that I saw him so much that summer when my own life had kited like a bad check. I would sit there with him and worry about myself and money, wanting a drink, seeing the dark bar top, the sweating glass and my cigarettes and a few dollars in change all neatly displayed like a table setting, with the back bar and mirror beyond in which I could study myself anytime I wanted.

Al was dying and I was too absorbed in such escape routes of my own to ever ask why he would shake his head like that, every once in a while. I would see him, and if I was sober I would be reconfirmed into my own fear for myself. I brought him candy which he wouldn't eat as an excuse for the fact that I had nothing to say. We would sit awhile until he would look at me and grin and whisper "son of a bitch" like there was some joke. I would grin like I got it. That's what this is, trying to get it.

For all the years I was a child, Al was a man who got up early and cooked his own hot cereal, and then was gone to build the fires in the California/Oregon Power Company blacksmith shop by six in the morning. Some of that, I'm sure, had to do with escape from my grandmother, who had become a woman driven to planning everyone's afflictions, and his need for some quiet and isolation before his long day of hammering at hot metal. He wanted his coffee and a fire and a newspaper in the early hours of breaking daylight.

Running away and the men he worked with had become habits too soon in his life, that was what my grandmother said, and I think she was glad to see him out of the house, and glad to see him home when he came off shift in the early afternoon, ready to work a couple of hours unmolested in his immaculate garden. So I'm sure that she understood that our trip to the Oregon coast was partly just his need to get out of the house. Maybe he wanted me simply for company, or maybe she insisted he take me, hoping he wouldn't do whatever terrible things she imagined if a child was along. No drinking and no desperate acts. Not that I ever saw him drink, but there were the old stories, like how he was drunk at their wedding, and kissed his mother instead of the bride.

It was early summer and foggy all day on the seashore, hot in the inland valleys around Ashland and Medford, and misty gray from the ridge of the coast range onward. We were in his new Chevrolet, bought the spring of 1939, as we drove down those twisting river courses. I recall the tidal flats and gray long pilings along the sod banks of the river, and great moored rafts of saw logs waiting for their trip to the mills near river mouth, where the rough lumber could be loaded onto ships.

"So there she is," my grandfather said.

In the oncoming evening we were parked on a headland with low rough surf breaking in on the rocks below, the sun descending into fog on the horizon. For a couple of days we just drove up and down through the little towns, staying in one shoreline motel or another, like he was confused about what he might be looking for now that he had stood on a cold beach with the foaming water slipping around his bare feet. One blowing afternoon we walked out amid the enormous dunes south of Florence and I climbed them and rolled down with sand in all my clothing while he watched my childhood like it was a puzzle. Then the third day we were north of Florence where the sea cliffs fall hundreds of feet to the breakers and we stopped at the place advertised as THE FAMOUS SEA LION CAVES.

Since then I have stopped there with children of my own. There are elevators now, which drop a little over a thousand feet to the caves. But in those days paths edged with damp red and yellow tulips led us most of the way down, the succulent groundcover edging to overhang above us as we worked our slow way switchback to switchback, the ocean booming below. We rested at the head of the boxed-in stairway, which was hung down the last crumbling wall of cliffs, where the cormorants roosted and circled their white-dripping perches, and the swirling haze broke open into quick and brilliant sunlight. We stood there blinking and rubbing our eyes like people who have always lived in caverns.

The sea looked to shatter in glassy rainbows as it rolled over great offshore rocks. The sea lions, maybe a dozen in all, played effortlessly through the waves, which lifted them and launched them onto the rocks, leaving them to climb to their perches. I hung on the railing with my grandfather clutching at the back of my coat, watching those great animals sport in water which swept them toward the rocks and breaking spray and then receded and came back again, until the fog closed over us, and we turned to go on down the staircase inside its box, with windows cut at the landings.

After turning and turning in that squared spiral, we came out into the cave where flickering lights led us down a dripping passageway, and entered the great cavern with its arched rock ceiling where the sea flowed through and the sea lions lived and fought and barked their indifference to us, living on the rocks and in the tides as if no one were watching.

There were maybe a thousand or so, and their din frightened me. Through a narrow slit of tunnel we could see out to the open sea, and I wanted to be there. In some side-angle way it all resembled dreams—my parents hundreds of miles away in the dry sunlight over the high deserts, the enormity of the cavern and those sluglike beasts moving with such assurance through the cold swaying water. We can only guess at what frightened the children we used to be.

I wanted out, so we began the long climb. At the beginning I ran ahead, and it was not until I'd spent maybe ten or fifteen minutes hanging out one of the windows along the endless flights of stairway that I sensed something was wrong. Al came slowly up toward me, gray-faced and drawn into himself, one step, and then one more step, resting, and then a few more.

It was then, for the first time, as he rested, that I saw him shake his head in that quick way, and pass his hand before his eyes as though brushing away cobwebs. I can see it now as a thing he learned to do right there, making his way up out of the Sea Lion Caves. When I had gone down to him, and gestured as though to take his arm and help, he opened his eyes and glared at me with what I took to be an expression of great anger. "Get away," he said, except he said it in German, the only German I ever heard from him, and he seemed like a stranger before he closed his eyes and went slowly down to his knees on the damp plank steps.

"Just a minute," he whispered, and he rested there.

He was carried the rest of the way by men who appeared to have been signaled by some miracle until I realized it was my weeping which drew them. They seemed to know what they were doing, as if this was something they had done many times before, and carried him slowly up in a wicker-seated sedan chair, step by slow step and then along the paths while he came back to himself and even smiled at me with what seemed enormous chagrined relief.

At the top he thanked the men, and they refused the money he offered, and we both sipped free cups of hot chocolate some heavyset woman brought us, two or three cups before my grandfather felt strong enough to get on his feet and make his way out to the Chevrolet, where it was parked along the cliffside highway. For a moment he stood with his keys in his thick hand, dangling by his side, as if he had forgotten what to do next, then he looked to me. "Ixnay," he said, our old game of pig Latin, and then he unlocked his door.

The summer I was thirty-five years old my first wife left to go live near her parents in California with our children. We were selling the ranch and I was terrified because my baby days in life were gone forever. The North American Van Lines truck had come and loaded furniture in the driveway. I was running the roads.

Al grinned as he listened to my troubles, like they were some joke we shared, and started whispering along about Butte and "three-dollar dogs," which turned out to be the meanest kind in his mythology. "They'd never turn you loose."

"That ought to be something," he said, and he was gazing away to the open window of the old folks home like it framed a scene in which some cheap savage curs of his imagining were hot on my ass, and it was funny. A couple of weeks later he was dead, of so-called natural causes. I never saw him again. By the time I got to his burial the casket was closed.

It's a quick story: I was shacked up in the Eugene Hotel when he died, with a bright thin woman who loved poetry, which seemed like grasping at straws to me. She made me sad because she wanted things there was nobody to give. There was no fuck like the one she wanted, ever on earth, at least as I understood possibility, and she showed me to myself as a fraud and a failure. So I made my excuses, and drove a hundred and fifty miles east across the Cascades to the desert country and the ranch and the empty house and threw out my sleeping bag on the living room carpet and suffered my way into the hangover that was coming, and then the telephone rang on the empty kitchen counter and I found out people had been looking for me the last three days. They were burying Al the next morning; the burying, for me, was pretty much a meaningless event.

What I imagined was Al blowing *charge* through his fist as the casket was lowered and my mother wept and my grandmother wept; I was the one trying to stifle his laughing there at graveside, whose life was the sadness and joke so everyone thought as they averted their eyes and I saw Al wheezing with good humor while I told him about shacking up in the Eugene Hotel, and my terror of that decent, wounded woman who wanted to try it one more slippery time. The King of France, he would say, if I had ever told him anything so true.

RHYTHM

by Jeff Hull

This is a story my father told me:

We had horses. My dad believed that caring for horses taught lessons about responsibility and life. As soon as I was old enough, I had a pony and started learning to take care of it, to make sure its life was comfortable and pleasant. This became a daily part of my life.

My dad had a favorite horse, a big bay mare named Rhythm. She had four black stockings and a jet black mane and tail. Her coat shined. So did her mane. It was like silk. She was a huge horse—seventeen and a half hands.

I never got to ride Rhythm much as a child because she was so big. But sometimes my father would pull me up on the saddle behind him and I would think that I was on the tallest horse there ever was. I used to think Rhythm was legendary. And my father seemed to tower when mounted on her.

They were both true giants to me. My father had straight and pure silver hair, even when I was young. (Although he'd never admit it, he was enough of a dandy to allow himself the lead-in to a ducktail.) He was a lawyer in a farm town and he had a very real and immediate sense of country justice.

But there's really no other way to describe him than severe. One day, as I came home after playing with Danny Wasserman, my dad said, "Come with me, young man." When he said that, it meant trouble. "Come with me, young man." I walked with him outside.

Dad walked through the backyard, past the toolshed and the rusted and blackened burn barrel. I had no idea where we were going. He kept walking, across the back pasture, through the far gate. Bugs filled the air.

We walked into the woods, along a path through the brush. Then the woods opened and a short, steep bank dropped to the river. The river was wide and flat, brown with mud. My father reached around and grabbed me by the back of the collar and a belt loop on my trousers and threw me in the river. He threw me in the river four times. I kept wading back to the bank and when I got close enough he'd grab my arm up high, slap a hand on my thigh, and heave me again. As soon as I saw him move I went limp, I let him throw me. The last thing you could do with my dad was put up a fight. So I let him throw me and I sat in the water until I got too cold.

By the end I was crying. I was cold and shivering, soaking wet with muddy water. It was nearly dark. I said, "Dad, I'm getting cold." I had no idea why he was doing this but I knew he would be doing it until he was done.

I said, "All right, I'll stay in. Is that what you want?"

He said nothing, he just stood on the bank.

I said, "Tell me what you want, Dad. How am I supposed to know what to do unless you tell me what you want?"

Then he turned and climbed up the bank, disappearing into the woods. I sat in the river and cried until I couldn't hear him anymore before I got up and followed. At dinner that night my father said, "Do you know why you were punished?"

I said, "No sir."

He said, "Tell your mother what you did to the Wassermans' cats."

I had no choice but to tell my mother, "We did like Dad did to the kittens."

Danny Wasserman and I had caught his family's two cats and carried them to the river in a burlap sack. It was a rough time, much different from when my father had done the same with a stray litter of kittens found in our stable. The Wassermans' cats were full grown, and clawed me and Danny through the burlap. We took turns carrying them, each of us holding the bag with both hands at arm's length. We added stones and dirt to the sack and threw it in the river.

My mother asked why. I told her Danny said they didn't want the cats anymore. I said, "We did the same thing Dad did with those kittens we didn't want down in the barn."

My father said, "That was different."

"How come?" I said.

My father dropped his fork, pointed at me, and said, "Don't you question me."

My father was like that about everything: black and white. He showed Rhythm at the county fair and they won showmanship-at-halter every year. He wouldn't braid Rhythm's mane or tie her tail, simply brushed the mane onto the left side of her neck and let her tail flow, full and jet black and glossy.

That big bay mare followed Dad around the ring like a dancer. He clucked and Rhythm switched her lead. My father didn't have to so much as lift his chin to stop her in her tracks, flat on all hooves. He loved that horse, but by God she did what he told her. The two of them glided around the dusty ring, the tall horse with its copper coat and jet black mane and my father with his silver. They were grand champions every year, until a young girl named Jenny Bird-low beat him.

The Birdlow girl showed a stallion which was high-strung and spirited, and her breasts stretched her shirt at the buttons. I thought she was really something—I wasn't quite sure what—until she won the grand champion ribbon. Dad never showed Rhythm again. He accepted the greenish white reserve champion ribbon and pinned it to Rhythm's halter and led her from the ring. He never said a word about it. In fact, the following spring he paid Mr. Birdlow to bring the stallion to our place for a few days to breed with Rhythm.

Mr. Birdlow came back for the foaling, too, and he brought his daughter. I was there and my father and Mr. Birdlow and my mother even came down to the stables for a little while, but she didn't stay for all of it. Jenny Birdlow wore a red halter top and her belly showed. Mr. Birdlow leaned with his forearms on the bottom half of the stall door and I tried to do the same but ended up with the wood in my armpits. Birdlow smoked a cigarette, too, and I thought, What a stupid thing to do in a stables. One stray ash and we'd all go up.

But nobody said anything to him about it. Jenny Birdlow stood beside her father. We were all anxious and we huddled and watched. My father knelt on the hay in the stall with his shirt rolled up over his elbows and stroked Rhythm's sides. He patted her rump. The horse lay on her side, her body bulged in a long copper mound. She made my father look small crouched at her hindquarters, but on her side, stretched flat out with her sides so swollen, she looked weak, frail.

Every time my father or Rhythm moved I could hear it in the rustle of the hay. At one point I pretended to wander over to say something to my mother. All I said was something like, "Do you think it will happen soon?"

I mumbled it, because everybody spoke in hushed voices while we waited. My mother said, "Soon."

But then I was standing right beside Jenny Birdlow and sneaking glances at the bare skin around her waist. She had jeans on and they were tight across her rear, but the waist floated loosely above her hips. When she turned her head I was quick enough to flick my eyes up to her face. Very quietly, so our parents would not hear, Jenny said, "Have you ever seen this?"

I said, "No."

She whispered, "I have. It's beautiful."

She seemed very sure of herself. But when things went bad, her father made her leave. It went bad quickly. My father and Mr. Birdlow recognized it at about the same time, when Rhythm worked and worked and nothing happened. Rhythm blew so hard I thought she would bleed through the nose. Her eyes bulged until they didn't look real anymore, but like huge brown marbles.

My father went in up to his elbows, trying to straighten things out. That was when my mother left. Mr. Birdlow sent Jenny with her. When Jenny tried to argue, her father said, "Goddamnit don't you sass me. Now get up there."

My father didn't make me leave. Mr. Birdlow asked my father if he thought he could save it. My father, who was on his knees and bent behind Rhythm with most of one arm up inside her, turned his head to look over his shoulder and said, "I'm worried about my god-damned *horse.*"

He scared me, because he seemed desperate and I could not imagine why. I realized something was happening that should frighten me, too, so then it did. There was black blood glistening on the hay. The whole stables smelled sticky with blood. Rhythm's breath wheezed deep in her throat. She lay stretched out. Her brown eyes bulged. My father worked his arm inside her. Blood squirted over his elbow. His eyes were pressed shut and his face sweated and his silver hair went straight even at the tips. He looked small compared to the bulk of the horse.

Mr. Birdlow asked, "You wanna just drag it on out?"

My father's arm slid from Rhythm and dropped to the hay. He rocked back on his heels. He said, "Hip's broke."

My father put both hands on his knees and leaned on them. Rhythm's eyes still bulged. She was frantic, only no longer moving. Her nostrils shuddered and her breath wheezed in her throat.

My father shuffled on his knees to the head of his horse. He grabbed her ear in his fist, leaned over, and put his mouth near it. He scratched the flat bone of her forehead with the fingertips of his other hand. Then he leaned back, patted her twice on the flat of her long neck and the second time he pushed himself away and up.

He asked Mr. Birdlow, "Do this for me? I've had the horse a long time."

My father headed for the stable door, scooped his hand to move me out in front of him. We all walked up to the house. My father stopped outside the back door to rinse his arm off at the spigot. At the house, Jenny Birdlow was in the kitchen with my mother. Jenny was drying our dishes. My father gave his shotgun and some shells to Mr. Birdlow. Then my father went into the parlor and sat on the davenport.

Mr. Birdlow went out the back door. My mother stopped me from going into the parlor, said she needed help in the kitchen. Jenny dried the dishes and I put them away. My mother finished with the washing and left. She went upstairs, I don't know where. Jenny and I worked in the kitchen and my father sat in the parlor. He was out of sight and silent, but I could feel him, as if he were standing right behind me. Jenny said, "What happened?"

"Hip's broke," I answered.

I heard a shot. It was muffled by the buildings, but clearly a shot. The screams ran right on top of the shot. They shrieked like vocal chords laid bare. Later I found out that Rhythm had jerked her head and Birdlow shot her nose and mouth off. The screams were hysterical, just raw vocal chords with the mouth shot off.

They came right on top of one another, the horse barely catching enough breath to scream again. Another shot popped in the barn, tiny, harmless, a firecracker under a cardboard box, but afterward everything was quiet except for vibrations of my father's footsteps on the floorboards.

It was so quiet I could feel his steps in the arches of my feet. Eventually I heard the springing screech of the screen door pulled open. I heard Mr. Birdlow say, "Jesus, Russ, I'm sorry."

I heard my father say, "I appreciate it."

Mr. Birdlow said, "Jenny, honey, come out here and wait in the truck now." Quieter, I heard him say, "Mind if I use your spigot?"

And I heard my father say, "Go ahead."

I heard the screen door slam shut. Then my father moving back into the parlor. I stood alone in the kitchen. I knew what had happened to Rhythm. I realized she was gone and I was heartbroken. I wanted to go to my father, and I wanted him to explain. I wanted to know why they had to make her scream like that.

I went to the parlor as quietly as I could. My father sat on the davenport. The shotgun lay across his knees, with the fingertips of both hands touching it. His head pressed backward and his eyes dropped to mine. He looked right at me and tears ran all over his face. I had never seen my father cry before. It was a thing that I had never thought possible. He looked right at me and wept.

I had wanted to go to my father and have him lift me onto his lap and tell me that things like this happened sometimes, that it was better for the horse. But the father on the davenport shocked me. I couldn't imagine sitting in his lap. He was different, I thought; as if he couldn't help me with water on his face. I backed away, and went out the screen door.

At the end of the drive I could see the red taillights of Birdlow's pickup as they pulled onto the road, then those were gone and it was dark. I looked down toward the stables. Thinking about the horse let me finally let go. I stood in the driveway in the dark, tasting dust that Birdlow's truck had left in the air, and I cried. This was the very first time in my life that I truly thought the bottom had fallen out, that everything that could possibly go wrong had or would and that nothing would be the same anymore and there was no explaining. I stood in the dark and cried until I got angry.

I got angry over the things that had been taken away, and I decided that what I was going to do about it was be a man. I was going to go down to the stables and start cleaning up the mess like a man would. I started toward the stables, deciding at every step to be a man about this. Crickets chirped all around me, some close and then others in the middle distance and even farther away.

The crickets seemed, to me, to be chirping in rhythm and their rhythm echoed and rolled away, far into the night as if it never ended. I was halfway to the stables when I heard the back door. My father yelled out my name. I didn't stop walking. I tried to hold my voice together and answered, "Yes."

"What are you doing?" he asked. His voice moved nearer.

"Stables."

"Why don't you wait right there for a minute."

I wanted to stop and I wanted to go on, to go to the stables on my own. But I stopped and saw a glimpse of his shirt rippling in the dark, then his silver hair, and I wanted to go on to the stables by myself, but then he was there. He touched my shoulder with his hand. He said, "You don't have to go down there, you know."

I was still crying but I wasn't going to anymore. I wasn't going to wipe away the tears already on my face, but I wasn't going to cry any more new ones while my father stood in front of me like this. Every single tear was going to be the last. My father's hand tightened on my shoulder, pulled me closer, but I didn't move my feet. I let him twist my upper body. My father told me, "It was the right thing but you don't have to do it."

I don't know if it was the right thing or not. The important thing was that he told me it was. And he didn't stop there, he kept talking instead of letting the silence build again. We walked down to the paddock and leaned against the fence rails and his voice came gently through the night. We both stared over the empty paddock and he started telling stories, quietly. He told stories about when he was young, what it was like growing up for him. He told me a story about his father.

IN THE COMPANY OF DEMONS

by David Seybold

When Richard Benson, the acclaimed American photographer and printer, told an interviewer he felt real freedom at not having had a father, that it must be very hard to have one, I thought I recognized a kindred spirit. Apart from a brief, and very unpleasant, period when I had a stepfather, I, too, grew up without a father, and I did feel a sort of freedom as a result. But one thing Benson said struck me most: that it must be especially hard to have a father when a son is in his twenties and thirties. According to Benson, this is because the son wouldn't know what to do with a father at that age.

When I was in my late twenties the fathers of my friends started to die, and I found myself grateful not to have a father of my own. To hear my friends articulate their relationships with their fathers—the love, hate, and regret—was enough to make me believe I was truly fortunate not to have had a father or know anything about him. Look at the sorrow I avoided. Every time a friend lost his father, I felt a wave of relief wash over me. For nearly twenty years it resolved a private dilemma of whether a son is better off knowing his father for only a short time, or not knowing him at all. Fatherless sons think about such things. They know the arguments for both sides.

There is a theory about sons without fathers that goes a long way toward describing my own youth. Not only does it accurately explain why I behaved as I did when growing up (like a sniveling ingrate determined to make people suffer for my being fatherless), it also made me realize I would have been better off knowing my father— for a decade, a year, a month, a week—a single day. Perhaps if I had known him for even the briefest of time I would have grown from the roots of a single, and truthful, heritage. As it was I knew nothing of my paternal past and felt compelled to invent one, which I did by lying and stealing bits and pieces of history from my friends. But the history I created for myself became a complicated puzzle with pieces that never fit. And the "freedom" I had by growing up fatherless was really a feeling of being anchorless and adrift, stranded on a raft in a rushing river that's approaching the open sea and all its uncertainties. Though in truth I was directionless and in far less control of my fate than my friends whose fathers were there for them, it was my early life's work never to admit it. Not even to myself.

The theory, originated by the German psychologist Alexander Mitscherlich, offers that when a boy grows up with little or no contact with his father, a hole appears in his psyche. Though it is a metaphoric perforation, what dwells in it are very real. The hole, Mitscherlich proposes, is populated with demons who actively disparage older men and urge the boy to follow suit. When a boy, who instinctively grows up seeking the masculine nourishment of a father, or grown man, despairs at his mentorless plight, he surrenders to the demons because they are present to enforce their powers while his father is not. All the while the boy grows, the demons encourage him to strike out against fatherhood and adult men. They say things like, "Don't trust or obey older men because they are liars and deceivers. Why respect them when they are never around to instruct, protect, or love you? Your father has abandoned you, left you helpless to fend for yourself while he is off in a place you cannot see or comprehend."

My father died in the South forty years ago. His death was sudden and unexpected, a shock to all who knew him. His body, already enervated by a rheumatic heart, a heavy-drinker's liver, and a smoker's polluted lungs, could not withstand the acute attack of bacterial gastroenteritis, a disorder causing inflammation of the lining of his stomach and intestines. Injections of penicillin, perhaps even sulfa treatments, were not enough to kill the virulent germs. They claimed their victim within days.

Specifically, he was on business in Baton Rouge, Louisiana, when the bacteria besieged his gastrointestinal tract. He was there to confer with his employers at the Ethyl Corporation before attending conferences in the Midwest. As Supervisor of Employment and Training Relations for Ethyl, my father traveled frequently from our home in New York, but would call every other night. When he last telephoned my mother, it was from the hospital, though he did not tell her. He did not say he was feeling ill and checking himself in for observation. If anything, he was slightly miffed that my mother wasn't in when he had called earlier. He wanted to know how his sons were, if Tom Junior was behaving, if I was sleeping through the night, if my mother was making progress settling into the house they had purchased only two months before. He said he was on schedule and still expected to be home in a week, that he'd call her again in a day or so. But then his fever surged upward, his abdominal pains became excruciating, internal bleeding commenced, and he lapsed into septic shock.

Not unlike most American husbands and fathers who are establishing themselves in the business world, my father tried to balance two lives. He loved his family, but was devoted to his career, which then was not yet a year old. Ever since his days as Assistant Director of Industrial Relations for the Cramp Shipbuilding Company in Philadelphia, where he worked during World War II, he had wanted to return to labor relations. When the opportunity arose, he resigned as vice president of the Dale Carnegie Institute and joined Ethyl, working out of its offices in Manhattan's Chrysler Building.

Because the bulk of his traveling was between New York and Baton Rouge, my father (unbeknownst to my mother) had made preliminary plans to move his family south in March, less than ten weeks away. Not only would he be closer to Ethyl's main offices, he would be able to spend more time with his wife and two sons. He intended to break the news of the move to his wife when he returned from the Midwest.

I have no photographs of my father and haven't seen one in thirty years. But I remember looking at pictures of him for hours when I was growing up. Even though I hated him for dying and abandoning me, I would go to a closet in the den and take out photographs of my father when no one was home. I would stare at them, searching for a trace of myself, to see what I had that would identify me as his son. His hair was thick and wavy, with streaks of gray that imparted a dignified aspect to his appearance. His facial features were smooth and well-proportioned, his eyes clear and confident as they looked directly into mine. (His was a classic, pipe-smoking handsomeness, the kind common in masculine advertisements of the 1940s and 1950s.) The feature I remember most, though, was his expression. In every photograph I ever saw, he offered the same slight smile that hinted at his being playful, a bit of a rascal, perhaps a flirt and tease. Now, so many years later, I recognize in my brother most of our father's features. In myself, I see a single visual link: the same slight smile.

No one from my father's company or the hospital where he had died called to tell my mother of her husband's death. She was told a few days later by a friend who had been contacted by someone in Ethyl's New York office. The woman, who had known my mother since childhood, called on a Saturday and said she and her husband would like to drive out from their home in Baldwin and visit the next day. My mother remembers there was nothing in the woman's voice to give away the shocking news she had to deliver. But when the couple arrived the next afternoon at our home in Stony Brook, a small harbor village on Long Island's North Shore, my mother saw the somber looks on their faces and knew something was wrong. They stood on the wide, wraparound porch bearing the burden of all the sorrow the world had ever known.

The cause of death would not mystify my mother. That part of it she would understand because of the nursing degree she earned when growing up in New Hampshire. What would be incomprehensible to her was the unfairness and suddenness of her husband's demise. Their life together was still new, with so much ahead of them. There was also the fact that her own years growing up had not been easy. Now was her time to enjoy life, a husband and family and new home. But knowing her, I imagine she mourned privately and let on to very few how she felt, living in a seemingly endless tailspin. Her New England—bred self-restraint and practicality precluded any outward display of emotions; she did what had to be done without complaint or self-pity. With her two sons playing about on newly waxed parquet floors, she made arrangements for their care and then made the long journey south alone to bury her husband. She was thirty-five, my brother five, and I five months. My father was thirty-three. Instead of moving to Baton Rouge that coming March, my mother remained in Stony Brook for the next three and a half decades—long after her sons had grown and gone their separate ways.

My father's name was Thomas Elwood Seybold, and he was born and raised in Newport News, Virginia. He had ambition, a strong will to escape his indigent childhood; he put himself through William and Mary undergraduate and law schools with money he earned as a radio actor and insurance salesman. He had a pilot's license, smoked a pipe, played golf, and belonged to community theater companies. He is buried in his hometown, in Peninsula Memorial Park, next to his mother, Laura Almond, and father, Albert Olivery.

I have never been to my father's grave, and I have no memory of him. What I do know about him has taken forty years to learn. It has taken so long because only in recent years have I tired of being angry over his death and stopped walking out of rooms and away from people when his name is mentioned. At long last I accept the fact that my father's early demise was no one's fault. I am willing to consider the premise that no one can breathe a moment of life beyond what fate has predestined. It may be so.

But the demons never go away. All through the boy's search for a father figure, his years of secretly, desperately seeking the love and guidance of an older man, they are still at work on his psyche. Even when the boy has become a man, the demons don't let go. It makes no difference how hard he tries to vanquish them, his entire life is lived in the realm of demons. Which is not to say he will never have any peace or forever be in their clutches. There are ways to live in the company of demons.

When the boy in manhood grows weary of his demons' incitements, the choice is finally his not to obey them. He can refuse to listen to their words of rebellion. And when the boy in manhood realizes the demons have caused him nothing but trouble all his life, the choice is finally his to say, "No more! For the loss of my father, the absence of his nourishment, I have made those who I love suffer with me because I could not bear to suffer alone. I hated my father for abandoning me and other men for not adopting me, and now I am tired and ashamed and will be so forever. Anger and bitterness be gone from my soul and never come back!"

When the boy in manhood feels these words staking claim to the tip of his tongue, he will begin to understand that all of life is an ever-changing series of choices. He will finally know that it's his choice to turn away from the demons and get on with the life his father gave him. Then the demons lose much of their power and are forced to retreat to the periphery of their host's psyche. There they howl and wail in voices that are thin and frayed and empty. At last they are only pests, nuisance reminders that dwell in perpetual darkness— the baying hounds of a fatherless soul.

LAST WORDS

by Dan Gerber

He motioned me down to the pillow where he lay in the intensive care unit. "I just want you to know I don't give a damn how this turns out," he whispered.

"I know you don't." I started to reach for his hand, then hesitated. It occurred to me that in his mind this wasn't one of the major events of his life but rather a sort of messy inconvenience that was happening very near the end of it. I had never seen my father lying in bed before, except perhaps very early on a Christmas morning when my sisters and I would barge into our parents' bedroom to awaken them to our frenzy of yuletide avarice.

There were tubes in his nose and a heart monitor strapped to his chest, and yet I had to restrain him from trying to rise in deference each time a nurse entered the room. Other than being treated for a shrapnel wound in France in 1918, my father had never been in a hospital or even in a doctor's office and didn't understand the protocol.

Several hours earlier my mother had called. "I think your father is dying. He's turned blue," she said. I raced the five or six miles to their house and arrived just ahead of the ambulance I had called before leaving home. He *had* turned blue. Congestive heart failure, the doctor said. His resistance to treatment, to having anyone inconvenienced by his condition, had been precluded by the fluid strangling his heart and, with a look that seemed to beg forgiveness, he surrendered to me and to the ambulance driver and allowed us to strap him onto the gurney. At the bend in the staircase his breathing stopped and, while the ambulance driver and I balanced him over the banister, the doctor plunged a needle into his chest and shot adrenaline directly into his heart.

The oscilloscope was the brightest thing in the room. Every few seconds an incandescent green arrow erupted and skittered off the northeast sector of the screen. My father and I were having one of those awkward silences we'd shared so often before when we found ourselves alone together, the same laconic spell I have since experienced with my son, like trying to make conversation on your first date with a girl you can't believe would actually deign to go out with you. I've never been able to figure out exactly why it's so hard to think of what to say, but I suspect it's because nothing can be taken back and because you respect and admire this person so much that you're always a little afraid of muddying the water between you. Or maybe it isn't that at all.

Once when my mother had taken up one of her self-imposed exiles in a Chicago hotel and my father had reluctantly followed her there, I took the opportunity, in a letter, to say some things I never seemed to be able to say in person. I simply told him that I loved him and that it had occurred to me that if my son ended up feeling about me the way I felt about him, that whatever else I did or didn't do in my life, I would consider it to have been a success.

A few days later he called, and through the interminable pauses he characteristically took in his speech, often waiting a full thirty seconds for the wanted word to occur to him, he thanked me for my letter and told me how it had made him think of all the men he had loved and how he wished he had taken the opportunity to tell them rather than telling someone else at their funerals.

I began to remember all the things I had said to my father, the things I had regretted because I feared, in retrospect, they would make him think less of me, things that caused him to sputter and flounder for a response, like the morning when I was twelve and told him that I thought it was time I acquired some sexual experience and suggested he should take me to a prostitute. I read a lot as a child, stored up ideas from books and believed they ought to be tested on life.

The nurse returned again to try to find a vein in his already needle-ravaged arms. He attempted to rise, and I restrained him with a hand on his shoulder. "It's okay, she works here," I said, glad for the excuse to say something even so obvious.

He looked down at his bloodstained, perforated arm. The nurse was taking up her tools again to try and torment him back toward life. For a moment he had the imploring look of a child, and I wanted to protect him. But from what? I'm not at all fond of needles myself, though I'd have offered my arm if I could have. A Zen master I once knew told me that the really tough thing about compassion, what makes it so important, is that in actual experience we can't take on even so much as a fart for somebody else. My father would have appreciated that. It's the sort of thing he might have said.

The nurse made several more futile attempts with her needle and surgical tube, and then her heart won out. "Okay," she said, "okay, we'll give it a rest."

I once had a conversation with a friend about last words. "Do you ever worry that the last thing you might say on earth will be something really stupid," he asked, "really inane, and that you'll see your life floating away and think, 'Oh no! I can't believe I actually said *that*!' " He told me the story of a famous restaurateur who raised his head feebly from the pillow and croaked, "Slice the ham thinner." And he told me how his father's last words to him came in the form of a precept: "Never eat a hamburger in a drug store," something Laertes might have heard before leaving Denmark.

I once heard someone say that many last words concern food. Eating is a pleasure—or should be a pleasure—we engage in several times a day, and if you don't take enjoyment in it, you don't enjoy your life. My father loved food. His letters to my grandparents from the trenches in France were mostly about food and the lack of it. He speculated about the pea crop in Michigan that summer, quipped that the only real danger he faced was from starvation, as they had the Germans on the run and it often took four days for their mess to catch up with them, and, as an afterthought, remarked that he had forgotten to mention in his previous letters that he had been awarded the Croix de Guerre several months earlier.

My father's last words were also about food. They came after another of those long silent spells and come back to me whenever I catch myself taking things a little too seriously. He motioned me down close again and whispered, "You know the only thing I'm going to miss?"

"No. What's that?"

"That spaghetti your mother was cooking," he said. He looked off toward the foot of the bed and smiled as if he could see it floating there in all its heaped and steaming splendor. Well, those weren't really his last words. I remember now that he did say one more thing, something that made me think of Orson Welles's "Rosebud" at the beginning of *Citizen Kane*, something I will never understand. He said, "You know, I think this is a blessing."

I knew what he meant, that it was a blessing he was going out like this rather than lingering on and becoming a burden. But just to prolong the conversation I asked, "What's that?"

His eyes swept across the ceiling and he smiled broadly, almost laughing, as if he'd seen something that pleased and amused him. "The Sky Raiders," he said. And then he closed his eyes.

I held his hand, feeling a little stunned by his inside joke. The Sky Raiders. I wanted to see this vision that he had found so entertaining. Maybe in time I will. I held his hand until it turned cold, and once the self-consciousness of life had fled, the self-consciousness of my life, I spoke freely. I said things like, "Well, what else is there to miss?" and "I love you, Dad" and "Don't worry, I'll take care of everything" and other things that didn't really need to be said, but that I needed to say, things I'm saying still.

NIGHT SOUL

by Joseph McElroy

The first night, the man woke to a string of sounds, expelled, quite awful stabs of voice throat-rasped, deliberate, from the crib across the room. So that for a time he felt the person there to be his equal, and he feared for him. In trouble over there, in a small, accurate way the infant is possessed and on his own, and maybe the man can't help his son, maybe he can't do anything about it. It is even part of *him* out of control.

A shallow-sleeping family man who will wake in the middle of the night anyway, he woke to the woman breathing next to him, and to the room in the desert, his eyes opening on the window at the foot of the bed, where the screen was ripped, burst, jagged as a wave with an infinitesimal fire—like steel or flesh—telling him something has gotten in here, an animal, a hand. While the terrible sounds from the crib across the room—*ah, ih, uh, eh*—choked out, cut off, not asking for anything, were vowels, he realized. As if this is what you do waking alone: You speak, even if you are not talking yet; for anyhow the room is awake. So that getting out of bed beside the breathing of his wife, he would make a noise the baby would hear—who would want his company, or hers. But these vowels uncannily at work, the child is choking or being taken away or accosting whatever it is, so what's his father doing here in bed? what is he waiting for?

Like a comrade he made his way across the cool bricks, he's with

117

his son in a moment—*flowed* there to him and stands above the crib in whose immaterial depths a blink of the mouth locates the face. Where are his eyes? Darkened, do they stare behind their lids? They're asleep in some way and distinct from the child that is his, whose mouth moves as the moon in the window above the crib draws a cloud in front of it. The kid's in one piece, thank God, thank the stars, thank the desert, but the sounds begin again, for they were no dream of the man's zigzagging away through low piñon pines and stunted, ancient-elbowed juniper the way the phone seems to have rung as you wake upon the waste of future and past that dreams are. But where are these sounds coming from if his son was not greeting a predator or giving a name to an intruder? Why, they're just practical sounds the baby's actually practicing, which the father hears as if his own good depended on it and will try to answer.

And so it happens that he is learning these sounds, like letting them strike what hasn't yet quite woken up in him: the *ah*, the *ih*. Squeezed off the palate hard, or choking, cut off, not hoarse at all in the dark but blunt, certain, and alone. The man's no clawed intruder but the father here, a witness; ready for anything—to be his son's equal, who is alone and launching these sounds, one that goes far, just the intent of it, while the next, you could swear, sends its breath at some near thing. Hearing is like answering him, even if they are no match for each other. He is to be answered. The man believes in it in the middle of the night. It's what he will tell him one day: Answer— not do what they *say*, but don't not answer. If tongue-tied, at least make a noise. Go *agh*, go *aiee*. Come back at them in a whisper. But don't not answer. Did the man just learn this, it feels so fresh? Seed planted in him in the middle of the night.

For the vowels are brave. They are things more right than words; but, as the man heard them, *there* and *here* are what they apparently say—*ah* and *ih*, a cast and a return; while the next, the *uh*, as in "mother," accepts what belongs to you, to this basic person, it measures just this. So to the man it meant, *What you found*; while the next, the *eh*, as in "again," *stops* what you found and holds it to what it is: *accosts* it; accosts what? the moon moving? a knife of reflected light cut by the ceiling beam? or a memory you can't have all by yourself? As good as an owl whistling in the arroyo, hearing like this, or some fool—hearing *there, here, found, accosting.*

The infant whispered like thought, old things are what he whispers into his thinking. The time has come, vowel cries that are about to come again that the man standing around naked in the middle of the night is learning, they are not to him, they are only what woke him. This creature in the crib talks out loud and with something at stake: but in an order more raw and stately—"*uh, ah, eh, ih, aw.*" *He* knows what he's doing—and to his father's ear it is *found, there, accosting, here,* just between the two of them a seesaw sense more *theirs* now, less to be feared.

Though hearing the *aw* sound hard and creaking as a bird, foraging and unconsciously alert, the man made little or nothing of it, and felt free to. So he stepped back so as not to wake the child with his body or familiarity; for if the kid is asleep after all, he could open his eyes that seem hidden by their lids from the darkness and the breathing of the man, and see the man, who now thinks proudly where this is, where they live—a desert state, vast or actually weird—"beloved," he likes to think, who, waking to the gash in the screen enhanced by the moonlight, forgot he already knew how it got ripped. Waking to these godawful sounds and the damaged window screen which his eyes told his brain was part of it, he thought *animal,* an animal had leapt in out of the desert. But no high-hipped bobcat far from its rock or lost bear cub or snouted coati with a taste for the fruits of the night that jumped out of somebody's truck on the Interstate is going to try a stunt like this. And in his heart like what he knew all along it was of course the same mange- and sore-ridden half-blind dog of yesterday who couldn't bear the noonday sky, the bright ground, and, wanting the shadow of the house, went for the open bedroom window while the family was having lunch.

His son's blood is safe from that dog, who wouldn't drink or eat and didn't even roll his eyes up when he brought two dishes in and then brought the baby in to show him this hounded creature, muzzle on the brick, too tired to have rabies or plague, where he had ended up collapsed with one hind leg out, the hide caked with adobe dirt.

A personal sigh has deepened the room, his wife's, and it threatens them with her perspective. She turns. She hears with her body, her mind, declines to talk in her sleep, hears her husband if necessary, yet will sleep on until, toward dawn, hearing the baby burst out crying, she will probably get out of bed in one motion, go and take him, hold him and nurse him. So the man knows from her breathing she is not doing any serious hearing of these sounds right now. Which come again in the moonlight, vowels in a whole *new* order, called and attempted, or brave; not crying, but uttered.

Plus the *o*-ish *aw*-ish one the man hears as *aw* now—vowel five, it's his.

They open to each other without at all getting mixed up together, to his ear like talk he hears in the kitchen of a Hopi farmer, a dog barking outside in the dusty wind of the mesa. Sounds coming your way, stopping short. *What was there is here; and now that it's found we accost it.* At nine months and five days, is his son at it already in a tongue of his own? What does it take? only the breath cut off in his throat that primitively rasps its old use. It goes back into him, a spirit—a way that's all his. That's what it is: his son's language under cover of night brought here from far away. But the man is the father, he's got too much at stake to let himself believe such things any longer tonight. Has he ever believed them? The *aw* pushes the speaker's lips, he knows them in his sleep. He pushes them across, so self-possessed by the nighttime vowels. *There, here, found, accosting,* was where the man came in. But then, *found, there, accosting, here.*

Are you all right? the woman murmurs more or less remote, as if she is thinking of him somewhere else. Mmhmm, he says, close to his son. Is it that his wife does so much, that she *feeds* the child? He does not envy her. Is it a madness in the infant's voice, which is only nature? And has the man ever believed such things as these coming to him in the baby's voice? He is aware of a long, winding, affirmative answer but it is going out of him somewhere else and he does not get it. He is going to know his son's language. It is a son's language. You can do that much.

It's changing, though, it's *"eh, uh"*—*accosting, found*—yet the known sounds *ih* and *ah* after them have changed their feeling to *if* and *dark, ih, ah*—with once again that *aw* which is little more than a neighbor sound following from the "dark" *ah* that's almost a stranger, an act. So what the man's getting is: *Only by accosting, you find—and only if dark.*

Thinking it, he can understand it, the baby at nine months old, years from such advice that comes best not from the father anyway but from elsewhere, from outside. Is it not from his son at all but *through* his son?—like how the man will speak to the baby (*You're* ready for a *nap*) but be speaking to his wife, the real other person here? The baby's mouth opening in the dark, or pursed; nursing the old life of these sounds, practicing it. But there's a thing somewhere the *man* has to do. Is it the *aw*? On his breath almost more than his voice, he says back, *eh, uh, ih, ah.*

The moon widening from behind a map of cloud stands harsh. Well, the man might be wrong but it's as if the mind of the probably sleeping infant thinks over what he just heard. There comes a startling new order, "uh" before "eh"—*found*; yet not *accosting*, but *again.* And *ih, ah,* but not with the feeling of *here, there* or *if dark,* but of a reaching, a stem. And *aw.* Which he thought was him, the father, taken down into what he might once have been—it shows him that these sounds might be not feelings or meanings. Does this baby blink at the moon, squint, not know the man leaning over the crib rail looking into the crib at him and the kicked-off blankets; or is he asleep?

The man crossing the room to go back to bed has his theory. It's his way of being crazy about his son, of not completely waking when he's hardly been asleep. The idea is that all this is coming *from* his son—it's not the child waiting to have something to imitate. It's late and not much of a theory; it helps the man hang on to the sounds.

Sleeping or waking he will go along with his son, who was asleep surely and the man heard him *talk* in his sleep as if it were himself for years and years. While during the next day the man didn't think of it much at all. For during the day, in overalls, the child watches.

You were up and around last night, she says. The man tells her he might have been sleepwalking the way it felt. You were standing at the crib, she says, did you cover him up? He doesn't think so. She tells him just how tired she was. *Go* on, he says, for she'll hear what he means, they accept her stamina and will try not to waste it. *Go on?* she says, but they agree, she will go on being what she is. You were talking again, she adds, meaning in his sleep. Are you sure? he inquires. Closing in on baby as if there's no difference between what she does and what the man does is the light of their attention powered by this chosen desert light let in by windows that belong to them. The baby, to whom the parents talk, sees them as if they're just talking. The man goes *grrr*, and, suddenly airborne out there at a height of six feet above the ground, the roadrunner, their rare, most serious and elusive, violently shy, narrow-bodied roadrunner, is seen to fly exposed thirty yards across the front of the house. While, closer, against the broad window sash of unfinished oak a zebra-tail lizard not supposed to be in the area comes into focus unseen by their son, who smiles, as if he's forgotten last night, and brags with a measured *Ha, ha.*

Yet at bedtime you forget that all day you've waited for when he won't be imitating his parents, but sharing a language of his own. And in the man's sleep it is the second night, and at the same hour the baby speaks out, nine months, *six* days.

And he's there for him in five seconds to find spread upon his son's nose and mouth like a flame of milk the pale seal of night light from a moon gone no higher than the broad southern sky but ready to go higher hauling indifferently this southwestern sea the desert, and the boy with it. Last night's launched vowelish tries go into each other with a speed of going *some*where, it's practice but it's a new night, it's not a thing he's saying or some outcry, but soundings. So last night's work is left behind with the man, as if the names his son needed have now been given—to the neighbor's wolf, the high call of the pallid bat feeding on the ground, faces of parents, the hand he examines in the moonlight with his shadowed eyes, the mobile that sways above an intruder's hand meeting the crib rail, the dog you expelled that the baby would not be surprised to see couched low on the brick floor. These names now made into raw orisons equal what's outside him, and the father can tell from the uninterrupted tone that the speaker is right. Is that it?

And for the instant that the man adds to his theory that what his son learned by hearing himself voice last night he now puts to use, the man nearly sees what he and his wife were really talking about, like almost recalling a dream he had on waking—but catches up with his son and with this old, direct way of doing things.

A joint tenderness of the parents—was that it?—the child who knows things from the very beginning? The man is not ashamed to hang on to it and to what he has heard in the night. Was *he* the intruder? Halfway to meet him he meets the baby's glittering eyes, and he won't back into the shadows. Nice person, he thought his wife murmured. Am I awake the way she is asleep? he thinks. He whispers his son's name: It means that the child has at stake this awful, right way of putting things together. Mammal messages able to evolve privately between beings. The crib a little less dark tonight, his smile asks nothing, not that he be picked up. His eyes *follow* what he is uttering because it goes somewhere.

When did the vowels grow these lids, these frictions and touches of maturity expelled with them from his palate, almost a *gh* before the *ah*, almost an *m* before the *eh*? The *aw* comes by itself still, but then is *gaw*, terribly alone like a watchman's warning, the *uh* has acquired an *m* after it, the *ih* finds a *dee* but the speaker is sticking onto the sounds the father learned and thought he knew, more than one sound, and the man hears *lah*, which he puts together with the *dee* to sing without song, and again this *gaw*, like another *go*.

The man, who's keeping up—all he wants is to know what the child knows. The infant isn't your equal, no matter how you try the strength of this talk. The infant is almost not there, dead you might say to this world, not a fit companion. Still, the man's idea is that these sounds now mix for work, and the child has sent them to a place away from him, and they join what they name or get stored in animals or what-all. Confident they've gone, he returns to the man, knowing him. You find a grin in the dark, and no complaint, no retort of, "You started it; you can pick me up." His baby son is unusual in that he has now closed his eyes, his night's work done. What is the father to do? Touch his wife and wake her? He hears his name, but just murmured at a considerable distance.

The brick floor cool as tiles is lower than the outside ground, and he stands at the window by the bed and looks through the ripped screen at the desert risen by another scale entirely. The man was closing in on the infant's way of sounding the distances between here and the life indifferently around him, no matter what the infant *thinks* he's doing. Aren't these older sounds a power that his son might for now give into his father's keeping?

It is the second afternoon when she says, You were whispering to him last night. *He* was whispering, the man replies. Well, you were, because it kept waking me up, she insists. But it was hard to hear, her husband goes on. But that's why I kept waking up, I had to strain my ears to hear; it wasn't like when you talk in your sleep, if I only got it all, the woman replies. Aw, you were asleep, the man tells her, never asking what she heard him say, though sometimes it sounds like predictions, according to her. You weren't whistling to the owl— were you calling to the ground bat again? she asks in friendship, it didn't sound like you what I heard in my sleep. It wasn't, he says. Maybe you were thinking out loud, she says to her husband. I wish I could, the man laughs. She laughs and then so does the baby, who *says*, more than laughs, *ah ah ah*, a baby in daylight. When are you going to fix the screen? she gets in as if this was what she really had in mind—don't do *that* in the middle of the night. *Gah*, he tells his son softly, *guh*; and *la-dee*, he practically whispers from memory.

The child won't answer, it doesn't work like that at this age— won't answer at all for a while. But then the man hears, *Mmuh mmuh*—the two parts it's made of. Is it word from the night shared by son and father now going toward day? You don't want what you said parroted back. Did you hear that? the woman asks. The man says he believes the baby's putting two things together. What things? she would like to know. This *uh*, he says. What *uh*? Something he's working on, the man reports. They contemplate each other, and contemplate the baby. Well, *I* thought it was "Mamma," the woman says. Could be, her husband grants. Is it precocious? she wonders addressing him and only him. The man, who might be losing ground, picks his wristwatch off the kitchen table, remembering the screen. What do we really know, he replies. His son says a short *a*, as in *man*—*a, a, a*.

Three nights, three foolhardy nights he and his son almost spent together on this. Waking, the third night, to the now invisible screen by the bed, dogs to be heard from the ranch a mile and a half away, and, as if still farther, the higher, thin-throated whoop of a coyote or two like answers of the land, the father doesn't hear the son; and then he does. The man has slept way past the middle of the night. What has he missed?

The phone ringing? Would that be his talking in his sleep, predicting things according to his wife? He's out of bed distracted for a second by a tiny fire a mile away, but it is his sleep still with him and with it names, a string of names. When did tonight's soundings begin? He can hear the baby's body. The woman breathes what sounds a little like, Hi. Sure enough the moon's in a new position, but through the crib bars the white-sleeved arms are pointing curiously and with that solitary power. Yet the man does not *like* what he hears so much. Less blunt, less certain. A nearly whispered "Da" does not mean the father, nor is it cut off or terrible. The eyelids are illuminated by the moon. His child is beautiful. There is a meaningless *gah* with some *rrr* of the day caught inside it. An old *eh* that accosts nothing but itself and is less like breathing than like a willingness. An *agh agh* that is in the dark and neither there nor anywhere except dreaming maybe of day. And a slow *ha ha ha*, and the *gaw* that was alone but tentative. And, without the *d*, another sound breathed with some prior seriousness the man's heart hopes for or asks something of.

From his sleep names flood him, animals, places. Along the horizon of the Jemez Mountains dawn could look like this line of sky to the west below stratus and, he thinks, altostratus cloud lids. Two horses in the dark lift their muzzles and are shadowy friends of the house some nights so that you see them best by not looking right at them, the rump of the paler Appaloosa obscured by the thick, dark little quarter horse. The half moon passes among the clouds and his wife makes a curved shape asleep but readier than the man, who has never quite heard himself talking in his sleep but has been dropping everything these last three nights to learn a language the speaker now may be letting go, or letting be, in favor of another.

And what *did* the man drop, that went away through piñons and juniper like a snake that wanted no part of you. I tried, he says, and the child rolls to his knees and sits up waking. Yes? the man says— but the child is not talking, he's getting set to cry and he cries terribly and piercingly, seeing the man: It means, You are not what I want, you are what I'm yelling at. The child, for the first time the man can recall, pulls up on the crib rail and stands screaming powerfully. And so it goes.

The man has seen the future and should find tomorrow night that his child has left him with elements no longer of much use and has gone on, although the man leaning down nakedly into the crib and lifting the child out now remembers when he dropped everything what it was he dropped. It was mountains far from here yet just out the window, a campfire, a dog, and two men talking. And he thought that if in his sleep he had put words to it he would see again who those men were.

So the three of them have been in bed for a while, the woman in the middle squeezing her breast from underneath to position the nipple maybe, the infant on the far side of the bed snorting quietly. He woke you up, she murmurs. We're both talkers, he says, on his elbow, as if he could stay disturbed and awake for good or slip back into shallow sleep. You woke me before you woke up yourself, you said his name, she says, but then you said "uh"—I believe it was "uh"—you said it a couple of times, you were asleep, as if you were thinking something, getting ready to say it.

The man obviously wants to speak, and he covers her breast with his hand. What did you mean, "I tried"? she asks, I thought you were speaking to *me*.

That it could wait, he says. Oh, good, she sighs. I said his *name*? he asks. She breathes. Maybe she isn't answering. Who on earth cares except the man? The child seems done.

The man might be angry, or talking to himself. Drop everything. Drop everything when he needs you, when he calls. And in return he grows up strong. If he needs you or speaks, if he does anything new, drop everything. It was what you were equal to. What did you get out of being equal to it? Well, you got the name of one of those men by a campfire. You're not really a night person, his wife goes on as if she's only half asleep, as if this answers what he asked.

Ask *him*, he replies. And with that he is out of bed and around to the far side and slides an arm and an elbow under the child and the other arm under the head so that his wife lifts her arm which was above the child's head and he takes the child from her while she turns to face the other way, her husband's side.

The desert bricks bring some later cold like a harbinger of daybreak against the soles of his feet, and beyond the window screen a scratching on the ground, a jackrabbit's claw, a neighbor dog remembering, is unanswered by the earth. You have to lower the child, you have to make it seem like there's no difference between your hands and arms and bones and the crib mattress, almost no motion from one to the other, these are the things that are necessary.

MY SON MY EXECUTIONER

by Donald Hall

My son, my executioner,
   I take you in my arms,
Quiet and small and just astir,
   And whom my body warms.

Sweet death, small son, our instrument
   Of immortality,
Your cries and hungers document
   Our bodily decay.

We twenty-five and twenty-two,
   Who seemed to live forever,
Observe enduring life in you
   And start to die together.

NOTES FOR A LIFE NOT MY OWN

by Verlyn Klinkenborg

In recent years I have written several essays in which my father played a part. They were allusive, as essays tend to be, and each one seemed to catch the feeling I was after at the time I wrote it. But even good work begins to drift away the moment it is done. Sooner or later every writer reaches the point where his words feel like a shroud. He begins to wish he could brush them away and step into the present, into the open, as himself. But to write is to commit words to the past, to build with bricks that finally conceal the writer, though the wall remains for anyone to see.

My father, at sixty-four, is still a young man in most ways. He and I use a language we have worked out for ourselves, a scientific language in which each word stands for one object. When we say "Montana" or "transmission fluid," we know what we're talking about. This tongue evolved in a disputatious time. My mother was our interpreter, and when she died we were left speechless. In the silent period that followed, I think we saw in my mother's death how much we stood to lose in each other. We have not talked about it. We have no words in our language appropriate to such feelings, though we know a thousand names for "trout lure." But this is true, and I say it for myself: Death makes individuals of us all. The individual it made for me was my father.

My father tells a story about a day in his childhood when he and his own father were making hay for neighbors in the northwest corner of Iowa. The terrain there is more exposed than the fields in Iowa's midlands. My father and his dad went home for the noon meal, and a storm blew up. When they returned to the hayfield, they found one man dead from a lightning strike and three men unconscious. They thought the four were sleeping. This is how the gods gave farmers silence.

My father tells another story. He and a friend had gone after whitefish in the high lakes of Colorado. The time was just before iceover, when the water turns black with cold. They were harvesting winter fish for the freezer, catching them with grubs on gold-plated hooks. As they fished, they huddled around a fire built on shore. A cowboy rode up on his horse. He dismounted, took a fishing rod from his gear, removed his boots, and wet-waded thigh-deep into the lake. He caught a short stringer of fish, waded back to shore, put on his boots, and rode away. This was one of the gods who gave farmers silence.

When my father cooks, he is likely to make one of three things: oyster stew, which he saves for Christmas Eve; chicken dumpling soup, which is a Saturday noon dish; or venison chili, which is made from last year's venison burger and carried frozen into camp. The recipe for venison chili he learned in elk camp from an old man who once cooked for Teddy Roosevelt. The trick is whole cloves.

I never knew the elk camp time of my father's life. It took place just before I was born, in the mountains around Meeker and Rifle,

Colorado. He was a high school teacher in Meeker. He wore his hair slicked back and smoked a pipe. He had a German shepherd named Prince, who disappeared one day, stolen. He corresponded with my mother, a nursing student in Des Moines. She was the youngest, by sixteen years, of the children in her family. Her brothers were old enough to be her fathers. She worried about the depth of her fiancé's faith. After my mother and father were wedded, my mother became the school nurse in Meeker. The only objects that I can date from that time are the head of a sizeable mule deer and the rifle with which it was shot. The deer was mounted in Texas and has watched over me all of my life.

A log house; the aspen and pine and timberline; a river with its own purposes, not a somnolent prairie stream; a dog; spring lamb, the gift of a rancher; elk in the freezer; mud-chinked ranch buildings; wild hay; the visits of farm kin, of parents; the ways of students, some bent against the path, some headlong down it; a child of one's own; the need for the child to have grandparents; a return to Iowa. So that when I grew older, old enough to walk through the corridors of an Iowa elementary school to the high school where my father taught, I could stand in his office, beside the bandroom, and there beneath the plate glass on his desk see photos of that time in Colorado, see a dog that had been stolen (and us dogless), see my mother, see my infant state, see the log house built on a raw scrape of land, all as if through a stream of clear green water.

My father tells a harvest story from his childhood in the northwest corner of Iowa. He always carried a .410 shotgun on the tractor. When a pheasant fluttered up from the stalks ahead, he would raise the gun to his hip and fire, one hand still on the steering wheel. He is as good a shot from the hip as from the shoulder. I have never seen it proved, but I know better than to doubt it. That is not the kind of thing he exaggerates. My first shotgun was a little .410 with an old-fashioned hammer. What was missing was the tractor and the cornfield and the birds and the solitude. We moved to California in the mid-sixties for my mother's health, but also because in Iowa the hunting had disappeared.

One night in Tahoe, a famous television actress invited a stranger from the audience to join her act. That was my dad. He cut the rug, sang harmony, danced with his arm around her waist. This is a scene a writer would like to embellish, but not a son. (The crackle of her clothing, the nimbus of perfume, the sex that seemed so personal from afar but was seen onstage to be a kind of ventriloquism.) When my father left the farm, he was led away by music. He played the baritone horn, the piano, and sang. Later, he directed. Sundays I would see him, back to the congregation, leading the choir with quick movements, the loose sleeves of the robe slipping down to his shoulder.

This is a memory I only hint at. In our small Iowa town, my father's high school band gave summer concerts. Townfolk gathered in the park near the swimming pool, its building gleaming like white adobe in the night. Down a slope lay the football field. The audience listened to marches and to popular songs. Once there was a party for band members on our lawn. The most beautiful women and the noblest men that I have ever known played in that band. But that was Iowa. In Iowa there was a track-and-field event called the football throw. There were watermelons in the yard and auroras in the sky.

If the temperature fell below 0, we could eat fried cornmeal mush for breakfast. When it rose to 50, we could wear spring jackets. Above 80, we could swim. I love to know the temperature. I have never met a farm boy who could swim well. They could strike a baseball cruelly, and they could play pinochle. Until I was fourteen, I never saw my uncles together without a card table between them. Their silence was not with each other. They had their own boys. There is not a single piece of his own good work that a farmer does with his mouth. Open it and out comes the weather.

From my mother I learned to make pie crusts and to iron shirts. From my father I learned to catnap and to tell time without a watch. My paternal grandfather spent most of my childhood trying to convince me that mustard was peanut butter and that peanut butter was mustard. It was a durable joke. He drove a push-button Chrysler and lived in town, which was as good as it got for an Iowa farmer. My maternal grandfather used to ask at breakfast if I was up for all day. He had failed as a tenant farmer and was retired by the time I knew him. His sense of humor never let him down.

The first time I heard my father swear, the word was "hell." He said, "What the hell do you think you're doing?" I was playing with a friend at the high snowy bank where the railroad tracks passed the graveyard. We had sent my brother home because he was cold. We lived two blocks away, straight back of the tracks, two houses in, easy, even for a kid. He had turned up frozen and had to be soaked in a lukewarm bath. My mother too almost froze to death as a child. She told of the sleep that nearly overcame her. As a boy I could picture the yard lights burning across the snow, too far away to reach, too far away to keep her awake.

The borders of character are permeable. I distrust any man who claims to have had a continuous friendship with his father. How did he get from fourteen to twenty-six? How well does he know his father, or himself? The disputatious time for me was the late sixties. I notice now that it was the one period of my father's life when he was cut off from the country. We lived in the suburbs of Sacramento, California. We fought over Ronald Reagan, over Janis Joplin. We lived in Iowa when the Beatles first appeared on Ed Sullivan. The whole family watched. The Beatles made a deep bow. There was John Lennon bending over his Rickenbacker guitar. I said, "He looks like Captain Kangaroo," and the whole family laughed. That laughter has burned in my ears for twenty-six years.

In the late summer of 1971 my mother died of leukemia. She was forty-three. She died after a ten-year remission, which she believed God had granted her—and who will doubt her?—so that she might raise her four children to an age of relative safety. I, the oldest, was nineteen when she died and callow, through no fault of hers, beyond my ability to comprehend it now. My father assembled his children on a bench in the backyard and told us that our mother, his wife, had died in her hospital room earlier that afternoon. Grief scattered us. But before we began to wander wherever our feelings carried us—we would bump into each other like strangers again and again over the next few hours—I happened to look at my father's face. It was the face, as I imagine it now, of Adam as he and Eve were led away from the Garden. With this difference: that Eve was the Garden from which my father was led away alone.

When we moved into the Sacramento house, it had two bedrooms, one bathroom, and a lawn. When we moved out, it had five bedrooms, three bathrooms, a new hallway, a new kitchen, garden, toolshed, woodshop, patio, child's fort raised on poles, and a doughboy pool. My father had erected a portable sawmill in the driveway. There was a trailer parked under the plane tree. There were chickens in the garden. At family reunions we pour cement. We do the work ourselves. I remember how modern, how Californian I felt when my dad remarried. We saw the honeymoon couple off at the airport and then we children drove ourselves home. They were bound for Oaxaca. Soon my dad and Sally, his new wife, will have been married for as long as my mother and father were married. Sally was as sadly damaged by death as my father. It is hard to say who saved whom, but both were saved, and the children were too.

And yet I remember the evenings in that last long summer of my mother's life, when we had not been told what our parents knew. She and my father left the dinner table and walked out through the backyard to a bench beneath the apricot tree. Sometimes they sat and sometimes they walked among the rows of corn and beans just past the grape arbor. Their movements were graceful, slow. Soon the delta breeze carried off the heat of day. We could see them there as we cleared the table, and we did not know what we were looking at. None of us was ever again so blessed by ignorance.

Now my father is rebuilding his childhood. He has an International Harvester tractor, fourteen acres of good pasture grown up in rye grass, a barn, and some cattle. The land is not as flat as it was in Iowa, nor as steep as it was in Colorado. I notice that I am rebuilding my father's childhood too. I have some pasture. I can see the use for some of his tools, the chain saw, the come-along, the winch. I remember the moment when I first realized that I resembled my father. Every son does. There is a spectral flash of recognition. Any woman you know sees the resemblance too plainly. I would like to be discovering now the ways I resemble my mother too.

The borders of character are permeable. When the gods gave farmers silence, they also gave them the power to mean great things by it. Words become a frail chattering on those prairies. As a boy, my father drove a horse team. An ancient metaphor for writing is derived from the movement of a team of oxen. The farmer walks behind them, clucking and singing. Birds hop in their path. The oxen bend to the yoke and in the earth a furrow is turned. The furrow is the line of words on the page. The page is the earth. The writer turns the team homeward. The birds rise into the sky and vanish.

THE FINE, BIG COUNTRY

by Russell Chatham

Above the ragged silhouette of the Gallatin Range, a sharp winter sun pokes through the stark fingers of cottonwood trees. The spring pond is still and utterly smooth beneath a brittle twilight. A dozen duck decoys rotate ever so slowly in the nearly imperceptible current.

At such an oblique angle, the sun allows no noticeable warmth beyond an illusion of it, and this lent only to the mountains by a wash of faded orange light. When the sun does disappear behind the ridge, the temperature will drop to nearly 0.

A lone hen mallard swings in from the river, winging hard, not slowing. Circling wide, it holds its distance and altitude while studying the decoys far below. As the circles fail to tighten, meaning the mallard is not buying the ruse, watching achieves a mesmerizing quality, which after some time fully replaces anticipation.

It is then, when I truly know that the mallard is not going to come within shooting range that I hear my father's voice. It comes to me as though from another room, and speaks about another lone duck that refused to decoy.

"That duck is never going to come in," my father says. And in his voice is a palpable sadness, one which implies a sense of loss concerning far more than a lone duck.

My father said those words the last time we hunted together, twenty years ago, on a gray, cold, and windless day in California right after Christmas.

We had left home at five A.M. and driven out into the delta country west of Sacramento, stopping off at a restaurant along the way to have breakfast. My father did not eat, only sipped coffee while I had a stack of pancakes, ham, hash browns, three eggs, toast, and two glasses of milk.

My large appetite caused us to arrive at the duck club late, and we had to lay out the three dozen sprig blocks in the light of dawn instead of the preferred darkness. We set the sprig decoys and got down into our barrel blinds and in three hours were circled by exactly one sprig. My father was right: That duck was never going to allow itself near the rice field we looked up from.

I remember looking at my father as he watched the sky for incoming ducks that would never arrive. I saw his beautiful hands holding the breech of his sixteen gauge Model 12, a shotgun he had owned all his life, and the canvas hunting vest he had on was the one he had worn since I could remember. It was the same vest he wore when he went dove hunting and fishing.

As my father watched the lone sprig in silence, I saw that his face was lined with a deep sadness that had been only partly formed when we used to hunt doves years before. Back then, before I was old enough to have a gun, I walked along with him and our spaniel Queenie and did not understand that it was the beginning of his sadness. Instead I admired his ability to shoot two, sometimes three doves before they were out of range.

There was a time when my father had been full of stories about the woods—not that he was what one thinks of as a woodsman; quite the contrary. But his words, if not entirely true, had the illusion of truth to them and were, at the very worst, harmless. The bluejay stays with the quail and warns it of danger; crows always post a sentry when they feed . . . This sort of thing.

On Sunday nights my father took all of us, my mother, younger brother, and two sisters, to my grandfather's house for dinner. He lived in the Sunset District of San Francisco, not far from Lincoln Park. My brother and sisters and mother were content to stay inside and sit and listen, but after a short time my father and I would look at each other and sense a mutual need to get out of the house. Then I waited for him to say, "Let's go for a walk in the fine, big country."

We would walk to the park, usually in the fog. It was not a manicured park with broad lawns but a tract of ground wooded with pine and cypress trees that extended from the Legion of Honor to Land's End and Seal Rock. We would enter the tangled forest and within minutes be worlds away from the city. My father would lead the way toward a clearing beneath the pines. Once there he would sit down in the pine needles and tell me to gather green twigs to build our house.

"Stack your lumber neatly and according to lengths," he would say. Then, when we had enough sticks, he would bend them in a half circle and push each end into the damp, soft earth, creating a sort of Quonset hut. The construction completed, he would sit back, light a cigarette, and in a somewhat distant voice say, "There's nothing . . . quite like . . . *the fine, big country.*"

On that morning when we last hunted together—when the lone sprig had flown off, leaving us to stare at the decoys from our barrel blinds—my father quit looking skyward for incoming ducks and turned to me, saying, "I don't know how you can think of getting married. I waited until I had ten thousand dollars in the bank. There are responsibilities."

"I'll never have ten thousand dollars."

"Of course not! You don't even have a job. What the hell are you going to do? You can't fool around fishing all your life. And don't give me that stuff about being an artist . . . that's the shortest road to the poorhouse."

"Doris is teaching college."

"I know. She has a real education. She's well read and damn

smart. What she sees in you is a complete mystery to me. Christ, you going to let her support you? I just don't understand at all."

"Maybe I could write stories about fishing and hunting. There's a market for it, I know."

"Don't be ridiculous. You couldn't even get through remedial English in high school. I worry about you. Get a job! Stop fooling around! Everyone has to do something they don't like. That's what work is. If you like it, it's not work."

We stared at the empty, leaden sky for another hour, then collected our decoys, returning them to their burlap sacks. During the drive home little was said, and I thought it best not to mention that my wife-to-be was already pregnant.

It is almost dark at the spring pond, and very high over the Yellowstone Valley ducks are flying in long, irregular Vs that constantly lengthen and shorten, expand and contract. They are mostly mallards that by morning will be in Utah or Idaho. The moon has risen over the Absarokas in a dusk moonrise, one of nature's most thrilling moments—so bluish and austere, yet full of warmth and promise even in this bitter season.

Even though I know no ducks will come into shooting range, I stay by the edge of the pond and stare at the last leaves of watercress. They remind me of the creek that ran through our ranch in the Carmel Valley.

My father always referred to the creek as the "crick." It flowed down the south slope of Mount Toro and emptied into the Carmel River. In winter steelhead would enter the river from the sea and swim upstream to spawn. If there was enough rain, some would leave the river and swim up the creek—almost as far as the ranch house—before depositing their eggs. When this happened, the "crick" was transformed into a nursery for baby steelhead that hid beneath lush beds of watercress.

When I was not fishing or hunting, I was sketching with my cousin. Each of us had received his own sketch box from our grandfather, and we would take these, along with a sketching umbrella, and set out from the house to spend the day drawing and painting. Often we would find ourselves on ridges high above brushy canyons, where sea breezes blew freely through scattered oaks. We would push our silk umbrella into the earth and sit in the shade of its perfectly diffused light and paint our pictures while the breezes from the ocean constantly refreshed us.

On several occasions my father went along with us and we urged him to paint. Though he tried a few times, he insisted he didn't like to do it, which now seems strange to me because he possessed an almost uncanny ability to draw. As a student at Stanford he had studied literature and art with more than average interest. He could recite volumes of poetry by heart, including Shakespeare's *Julius Caesar* in its entirety, and had saved dozens of his drawings and pastels, which were enormously sophisticated, beautiful.

When I was younger, perhaps five or six, one of my biggest thrills was to ask my father to draw something after I went to bed. In the morning I would awake and rush into the living room to find a drawing in his chair. I don't recall any Christmas morning being as exciting as those when I knew there would be a picture waiting for me.

By nature my father was a gentle and quiet, even reclusive man. He had no greed and was not interested in possessions or money beyond what would make him and his family comfortable. And even though he carried a feeling all his life that his older brother had tormented him (because of an illness that had rendered him sickly and underweight when he was a youth), he still went into the family lumber business with my uncle when he graduated from college.

It was called the Loop Lumber & Mill Company, and it had been founded by my grandfather and a partner in 1855. With one yard on the San Francisco waterfront and another on the Alameda Estuary, it was one of the Bay Area's largest and most successful lumber companies. But in 1954 the ninety-nine-year lease, held by the Southern Pacific Railroad, ran out on the San Francisco yard and was not renewable. My father then commuted daily to the Alameda yard, which was managed by his brother, and sat at a desk where he calculated board-foot prices and maintained a tally of the yard's inventory.

I had been told there would be room for me at the Alameda yard, if that's what I wanted. It was not what I wanted, though, at least not for a career. But I did work there for a number of summers, mostly in the cabinet shop. And after I was married I continued on a part-time basis. I stacked lumber, maintained the buildings, loaded and un-loaded delivery trucks, fed and tailed-off the planer, drove the Ross Carriers, filed saws, built custom windows and doors, and painted signs. I loved the mill and its vast sheds of fine woods and ancient, soulful machinery. But the thought of me making the lumber busi-ness a career was extremely remote.

In 1939 my father earned a thousand dollars a month, which made us rather well off. Thirty years later he was still making the same amount, which meant that for three decades he had taken an annual cut in pay and was earning less than a union laborer. By the early 1970s the Loop Lumber & Mill Company, which had been operating unaltered since the 1930s, was losing money and forced into Chapter 11. The beautiful yard was demolished and replaced with some sort of shopping mall. For his years of service, my father received a Social Security check that was too small to cover the taxes on his house.

It was, I now believe, when I started high school in 1954 that my father, who was forty-seven years old, lost all control over his own destiny. I don't think it had anything to do with the lumber business, though, because the yards were lively, fascinating places, and there's no question he enjoyed the ambience. For reasons I cannot explain, my father no longer found any sense of personal satisfaction in his job, and he lacked the drive to look for it elsewhere.

In all the years I knew my father, he never varied from his daily routine: He went to work at seven A.M. and returned home at six P.M. Upon arriving home, he started drinking and by ten-thirty or eleven was sound asleep from having drunk half a bottle of bourbon and a bottle of red wine. Though he never appeared particularly intoxicated, he also never showed any sign of receiving release or enjoyment from the alcohol. And it was then, when life held nothing for him but work and paying bills, that he began to sink more deeply into his own dark shell, cutting himself off further and further from the life that revolved around him.

One day, to my horror, I discovered that he had destroyed all of his drawings—all of the beautiful sketches and pastels that I had loved so much. When I asked him why, he simply said they were no good and that burning them with the rest of the trash was the right thing to do. I searched the basement again and again, hoping he had missed a few. But I never found any. He had destroyed them all.

Only after I had married and fathered a daughter and moved to Montana did my father resign himself to my style of living, which to him seemed largely indigent. I had no job, owned no property, had very little money, and drove used cars. I had indeed, as he had said so many times, found the shortest road to the poorhouse. Even so, I remained resolute in my belief that life was to be lived and not merely endured. The hunting and fishing I enjoyed as a youth had become integral parts of my adulthood—unlike my father, who considered field sports lazy escapes from reality, a reality that for him consisted of a nightmarish cycle of bills.

It is nearly dark now and the Absarokas appear as a dimly lit stage set against the violet light. Shooting time is over and I unload my shotgun and lay it in the snow. The decoys are indistinct in the fading light and I know that the geese I hear high overhead will not come in to the spring pond or river beyond. They will continue on their way, flying unseen through the descending darkness.

I went to San Francisco to see my father when he became ill. He had been operated on for cancer but was told there was little chance the operation would actually help.

When I reached the hospital the nurse said he was in physical therapy and that it would be all right to visit him there. I remember feeling rather nervous as I stood looking about for my father. Several patients were struggling with walkers and other devices, and it took me a few moments to pick out the thin, hunched figure in a wheel-chair who was staring in my direction. When I looked at him, I wanted to turn and run.

"Russ?"

"Hi, Dad."

"Jesus, don't you ever get your hair cut?"

An efficient, heavyset nurse wheeled my father toward me.

"Russ, this is Mrs. Wilson. Mrs. Wilson, this is my son, Russ. He never gets his hair cut. I didn't even recognize him. He just looked kind of familiar, so I took a chance and got lucky."

I hadn't recognized my father, either. He had lost so much weight that he appeared almost skeletal. But most noticeable of all was that the despair and frustration were gone from his face. His sadness, too. Even his anger, which had hovered so constantly over his every move and which I had always taken to be at least some sign of life, was gone. What was left was nearly an absence of matter: complete resignation, complete acceptance that his life, such as it had been, was over. He stared vacantly at a spot somewhere between the wall and the floor. He seemed embarrassed.

"I can't believe this is happening to me," he said.

"The doc says you're doing great."

Mrs. Wilson wheeled him back to his room and I followed. I sat with him for a while and we talked about things that had happened long ago and were never mentioned since.

"Remember when we used to catch the crawfish in Lagunitas Creek? You'd always take me over there on weekends and we'd bring a bucketful home."

"Yeah," he said, "I remember. You were always afraid of them."

"I still am. But you know what I remember most? It was the Saturday I was sick and couldn't go along. You caught that big trout we'd seen in the hole a couple of times before. Must have been a small steelhead that got stranded there for the summer. You caught that trout and I wasn't there to be a part of it. I felt like I had missed the most important thing that ever happened. I think about it every so often. It helps me to know that I don't ever want to miss anything again if I can help it."

"You need money?"

"No," I said. "I'm fine."

"I hope you don't need money because I'm pretty short myself these days. I worry about you."

"Don't, I'm fine. Really."

The moon glints brightly off the surface of the spring pond as I pick up the decoys and return them to the sack. It is very cold, and I realize that despite my many years of living in Montana, the weather here is still a shock when you've been born and raised in San Francisco.

My father has been dead for more than a year, and it sometimes seems shameful to me that I don't miss him more. I loved him so much but never told him, and he in his shell of despair was never able to say he loved me. What he said, or rather expressed, to me was his fear of failure. He wanted to discourage me from trying to do anything, believing subconsciously, I think, that he was protecting me from the pain of the failure that he was certain awaited me. But I only wanted him to say he loved me.

When I look back now, I wonder more than ever what caused my father's sense of reality to change. What could have happened to turn him away from a life filled with poetry, drawing, ducks, doves, trout, crawfish, and walks in the park, to a cold and pointless one that was filled with accounts due and receivable? When did despair and anger replace hope and happiness? Why did a life so potentially rich become so psychologically and emotionally abbreviated?

Still, as I walk through the moonlit mountain night, far from the sensuous California landscape that I was born into, I can sense my father walking with me in this fine, big country.

THE BUZZARDS

by Sydney Lea

Looking across Swamp Creek from my grandparents' meadow, I could count on finding them. I'd seen one or two from close enough range to know they weren't handsome. Yet I forgot that as I watched the simple ease of their drifting over the opposite ridge, so lovely I'd behold it for hours. Or more likely I *imagined* the passage of hours— all time moves lazily for a child on summer vacation; no doubt that's why I still associate the glide of vultures with a lost, languorous innocence.

My memories of the grandparents are vague, scattered: a snatch of talk here, a gesture or two there. They were gone early, and their house in Sumneytown, Pennsylvania, devolved to my father. It has since passed on to others, and Eastern megalopolis gulped its once wild surroundings. While Dad lived, however, it seemed a genuine backcountry retreat. Though the word didn't fit even then, we called it the Cabin.

My father's father had dammed Swamp Creek at the foot of his meadow before any of us grandchildren—three brothers and, eventually, two sisters—was born. We'd soak in the swimming hole till our fingertips wrinkled and blued. Then we would walk or paddle upstream, where the water ran through a great boulder field. Like all child societies, ours had a pecking order, and each family member or friend's position within it was established on the Rocks, as we artlessly called them. How rapidly could we improvise a way from this boulder to that? How wide were the chasms we dared to leap? Our play inevitably resulted in painful abrasions, but barring any worse injury, we'd carry on full speed till exhaustion overcame us.

Afterward we'd lie on a level slab we named Flatbed, from which we could also see those sailing buzzards. And as the rock warmed my bones and my breath slowed, I always imagined my father's presence, no matter where he physically was. I'd look through slitted eyes at the birds in their cycles, steady and effortless as earth's, and at length could imagine gentle revolution in my own being.

I am the eldest son of an eldest son, and named for him. In remembering my father, I long to establish profounder symmetries than these obvious, factual ones; yet every effort feels instantly compromised by his early death. Sydney Lea, 1909–1966: To think of that terse message on his urn is to imagine the abrogation of some deep *formality* between us.

At over six feet tall and two hundred pounds, my father looked imposing. But his slowness to anger was almost perverse, or so I sometimes thought. Enjoying (the word is exact) a reputation for gentle judgment, he was also known for sympathy with players against long odds, from fellow businessmen down on their luck to the pioneer blacks, as I'm especially proud to recall, of the modern civil rights movement.

I associate my father most fondly with the outdoors. Unlike mine, his was never a character to be positively *consumed* by a passion for woods or waters or gun dogs. I confess I now and then held this against him too: If he insisted on doing so many other things with integrity, why be casual with these? In that much more calm and casual fashion, however, he loved these things I love, and he introduced me to them early. For this, at least, I am grateful.

Most of my reactions to his death proved a lot messier. Among them was a peculiar fury, as though this time tolerance had gone too damned far, the way for example it often had with an unruly dog; as though my father had given too much of his famous big heart. He should have shown who was boss. To whom? Well, to someone, even if that wasn't his style.

After the funeral, as I stood staring at a few nothings returned by the hospital staff—my father's watch; his ungainly steel pocketknife with the crescent wrench at one end; $1.09 in coin—I recognized terror in my responses too. Suddenly, at twenty-three, I was not only mortal but also unprotected: Ever the hothead, I might curse my father's tolerance, but it had after all blessed me, however incompletely I'd felt the blessing till now. Inseparable from such feelings of deprivation, though, was another feeling, dim and painful at once: I was henceforth fated—a bit like Coleridge's sailor, but well before reaching his age—to tell a tale that would never be quite complete.

It must be late summer of 1952, my mother big with her first daughter, my first sister. Why else would she stay at home? The two younger brothers are somewhere else too: I can't say where, or even care, my own wonderful circumstance crowding out such trivial detail. I've come to the Cabin alone with my father, a treat so rare that a noble truth has the freshness of discovery: Dad knows when and when not to be on hand.

Since breakfast, he's been working in the squat little smokehouse. The building lost its original function before I ever saw it, and is now a kind of guest quarters whose plaster needs whitewash. I haven't been asked to help. I've been set free to swim all these hours unattended. No other parents would leave me to such happy devices: They'd worry about drowning, or maybe even snakebite. My father is above such ignorance; like me, if more quietly, he holds it in some contempt. A father to be proud of.

At about ten-thirty I dog-paddle—a fair swim and most of it over my head—to the Rocks; but I'm not inclined to play up there by myself. Instead I flop down on Flatbed to watch some half dozen buzzards, riding the updrafts over Finland Ridge. Each follows each in a circle, the first one dipping out of sight on the far side, returning just as the last disappears. I close my lids when that lead buzzard drops behind the hill, and try to open them exactly when he sails back into view. Though it works for a spell, I finally shut my eyes and forget to reopen them.

Coming to, I blink, the taste in my mouth telling me I've dozed. The buzzards are still in the same formation. As I get to my feet, a green heron startles me, squawkily flushing close by. It lights in the brown ash above Serpent Rock, and I wonder if a heron might eat a snake. I hope not. We like to peek into the boulder's cleft, my brothers and I, because we can rely on finding the snake at home. Although we often poke at the poor thing with a stick, it never comes out, only hisses and jets its stink (which is horrible but seems appropriate, almost attractive). Father frowns on such play, explaining over and over that we court no danger, as we prefer to think. Rather, we inflict terror on a defenseless being, and ought to be ashamed.

On Flatbed, I feel a moment of soft breeze before I slide back into water whose warmth by now so nearly matches the air's that I scarcely notice the change. Invisible current carries me all the way to the sluice in the dam's apron, where the usual tiny sunfish— pumpkinseeds—nibble at my toes.

An ordinary day, then, but an extraordinary situation: How fine it is to be half on my own, free at least of the younger brothers who forever dog my steps at the Cabin. Not that I resent their company; only that in its absence I can do as I want, undistracted, all but a man.

Walking up through the meadow, flushing rackety grasshoppers, I discover that what I really want is food. Yet the sun's still well east, and I sigh, knowing I'll have to wait out my father's work. Having taken on his job, he will proceed with maddening patience until it's done. I turn into the woods just shy of the porch, making for the springhole we call Frog Village.

But how long must I stay? Likely a good while. I forget about my own hunger at any rate, forget even to expect the low moan from the conch shell, my father's familiar summons back to the Cabin—a sound so mellow and full of liquid glissandi that we children always take our own sweet time responding to it.

It isn't the horn I finally hear, though. It's the fire bell, and my neckhairs stand. Nobody, adult or child, is allowed to ring the bell except in emergency. For all the days I have spent here, I've heard it only one time, when Uncle Roy's springer spaniel Speed was bitten by a copperhead. I suddenly recall how frantic and frightened we were, at least the children, piling into the wood-paneled Chevy, Speed's paw swelling more grotesquely by the minute, the closest vet way off in Green Lane.

Breathless, I reach the Cabin, where I'm instantly relieved, and thrilled. My father takes me by the shoulders and steers my gaze across the swimming hole to an incredible descent of vultures to the top of the ridge.

He doesn't need to say anything. I gallop close after him over the field and the dam and up the hillside, so driven by wonder and curiosity that the quick climb seems easy. Still and all, my father is soon well ahead of me. When at last I duck under a soft, out-of-place willow and come through to the other side, he's already among the buzzards. Behind him I can just see the heavy-racked whitetail buck that has drawn them. Even in death the animal seems—self-contained. He's an unusually dark deer, almost black, with a pure ebony strip from withers to flag. Though it's late summer, the buck's antlers still trail a grizzled rag or two of velvet, but by contrast to its coat the horns look phosphorescent, ghostly. The sun strikes his upside eye; it crackles like a sparkler.

A string of vultures perches in the hemlock stand at the far edge of the clearing. I sense more than see them, intent as I am on the fallen deer. And yet I feel somehow that the birds, too, are part of a composition whose foreground is commanded by my father. I want to enter the picture, and take a step or so in his direction, but he signals me back with a flatted palm. In the instant, my attention swinging to that big hand, I believe in his ability to arrange things however he chooses. In fact I imagine that he has already done so, that in some way he keeps me off not for fear of my reactions but of disturbing an exquisite rightness, the balance he has willed into being. The deer at my father's back, larger than any I've seen, is small compared to him. Even the vultures' high hemlocks shrink as I look on.

Though I know in my soul that the buzzards will have at the dead buck again, which is as it should be, it's a stasis that will linger in mind for years: My father, turning, raises his arms like a prophet; the buzzards take to air in their hundreds, climbing and climbing till at last they resume their slow cycles in the sky, full of familiar grace.

Here's another version:

My father and I are the only ones here, and he's been busy. He still is. I can picture him in his baggy, whitewash-spattered shorts, cooking inside the Cabin. Alone and bored all morning, I'm looking forward to lunch as a relief, however temporary or minor. Why must everything take so *long*? The frogs are stuffed: I've caught one bug after another for them, and they've lost interest. I watch the surviving mayflies kick and twitch, and I wait for the honk of the shell.

When I hear the porch bell instead, I don't think to worry. I think: Something's up. I come in a rush, low softwood limbs abrading my face and spider-silk gumming it. But there isn't any disaster waiting. Dad's pointing at Finland Ridge, where the buzzards are thick as roost-bound crows.

"Let's go see," he says, his eyes shining the way they do, some-times over the smallest matters. He makes for the dam at a kind of dogtrot.

I've watched vultures land on the ridge often enough, but never, it's true, in numbers like this. As I catch up with my father, I catch up with a little of his enthusiasm too.

The woods on the far side of the creek are dense in any season, but especially summer. They make slow going, and it's a hot, hard climb up the flank. When I pause for breath in the clearings, I can see straggler birds luffing down through the canopy at the spot we mean to reach. But the spot doesn't seem to get closer; I begin to feel that it's actually *receding* as we move. My small excitement fades, and I also begin to feel like quitting. I whip my poor body on, though, trying to believe in a purpose beyond the mere discovery of what some vultures are up to. Trying to believe this is what's called man's work.

At last I crawl under a cedar, scratching my face again on dry lower limbs, and my palms and knees on the spills. When I straighten up, I see the full flock. It's a huge, black, filthy swirl, my father standing on this side of it, his shirt soaked, his mouth gapped for air, his glasses clouded with steam. He looks balder than I remember, dumpier.

It's a long spell before I can take my eyes off him. Winded as he is, he keeps trying to light a smoke, but his hand shakes and he drops his Zippo again and again. When he finally goes down on his knees to grub for it, I look away to the buzzards. They're swarming a cowhorn deer, its little tines crusty with old velvet, its hamstrings ruined. Dogs, I figure. We don't have any other predators to manage the job. Is it those rotted hindparts I smell, or the birds themselves? I'm surprised by the *sound* of the vultures, something between a cluck and a hoot, like barn owls on a rafter. At this close distance, the sheer ugliness of the buzzards also surprises. And how much smaller they seem than I've imagined!

Young as I am, I've been a hunter for two years and seen a fair amount of blood; yet the sight of the young deer, maimed by the dogs and now by the buzzards, revolts me. To think of its suffering! Couldn't it have outrun a pack of fat pets? I retreat some. So does my father; but when he reaches my side he suddenly appears to have second thoughts and walks unsteadily back toward the carcass. Sure enough, like their Hollywood cousins, the vultures hop only a few yards off. They shoot their necks and gawk; they hum and cluck. I don't know what my father's designs are, either on bird or buck. I don't really want to know.

Scrambling and tumbling down the hillside, I fetch up at the dam. Directly south, the sun turns the color of a tin cup, and I feel the first drops of gray, tepid rain. It's only a minute or so before my father joins me. His chest is still heaving, and he doesn't say a word. Holding his fogged eyeglasses in one hand, he squints along the apron for a few moments, then, feeling with his soft moccasin soles—as one might do to cross a room in pitch dark—he walks to the other shore, a step at a time.

I follow. Both of us silent, I can hear the silly gabble of the buzzards, feasting in the high woods. To block the noise, I start to whistle tunelessly. The swimming hole is scantly pocked by rainfall;

at the sluice, the usual trash fish—bluegills and sunnies—face me just under the surface, rounding their white-rubber maws, hoping for a crust, or even a crumb.

In our absence, the hamburgers have gone gelid and beady, and in any case Dad and I are short on appetite. We scrape the meat into a paper bag, to be dropped off at the dump on the way home. For now my father wanders into his bedroom, and soon his irregular snores sound from behind the door.

Left on my own, I take up a Red Ryder comic book. I read the accounts of Red's triumphs, first to myself in silence and then again and again, louder and louder, stressing each *pow!* and *bang!*—as if to wake my father.

Now, almost forty years later, I'm lugging my five-year-old son in a backpack up the steepest side of Stonehouse Mountain, New Hampshire. It's the middle of June, a gorgeous day, the leaves the size of a fox's ear, the woods going green out of gold.

There are no buzzards here, old or new; but there is a boy. He has so much ahead of him now, and I so much behind. Yet there are other and brighter auguries too: I'm in damned good shape—a lot better, I suspect, than my father was at this age, just a decade short of his death—and I'm lucky to have so much beauty outside my very door, pure in its different way as the beauty around the Cabin, before the changes.

I've labored for thirty minutes to reach this ledge. We call it Flying Squirrels because once, in winter, we flushed a crowd of the things from a holey white pine at its top. Their soaring was a wonder, carrying them clean out of sight down the flank of the mountain. Thus, as places sometimes will, this one now strikes us as almost sanctified. If the squirrels have never been seen again, still the spot remains rich with promise as well as recall.

But I summon myself back to matters before me. My burden is precious, I must take care, I will pick my way with both hands and feet here. When I grasp the final outcropping and pull us onto height-of-land, I nearly touch the fawn who lies in a stone hollow.

As it jumps and goes, I can almost feel my little son's eyes widen behind me. "Look!" he bellows. "Look! Look! *Look*, Dad!"

The fawn bounds north along the monolith. Reaching the drop-off, it poses side-to. Perfect, all this: dark evergreen in the near distance, four pale rivers of lingering snow on Mount Moosilauke in the far, the music of deepwoods birds all around us, and the smell of new mud and fern. We watch for another few moments before the little deer steps gingerly back our way, close enough that its white spots come into focus again. We see its delicate nostrils, flared by caution. Then it bolts, leaping a juniper clump and dashing down into black swamp eastward.

I clamber on a few feet, and stop. We hear the rustle and splash of the small beast's going, and at length, I think, the unseen doe as she searches it in the brush. Nothing and no one around me is really dead. The child on my back will ride me till we're home. My chest heaving, my glasses fogged, I stand till he urges me on. I suppose he'll want to tell the story of this scene—and of his father's part, or parts, in it.

MY FATHER'S SON

by Jim Fergus

My father, Bill Fergus, owned a Ford dealership in Skokie, Illinois. Fergus Ford. I am told it still exists with the same name, although my father has been dead for nearly a quarter of a century and no one from our family has had anything to do with the business since. Now there is even a Fergus Datsun. How strange my father, a veteran who was in Japan at the end of the war, would find that.

Sometimes in the summer, my father would take me down to the dealership with him. I loved cars, loved hanging around talking to the mechanics and the salesmen and the receptionists. For lunch he took me to a wonderful roadhouse restaurant. It was dimly lit by candles, and had starched white tablecloths. My father went there every day for years, and of course everyone knew him. He had his own table. My father smoked Camels, and at lunch drank two Beefeater martinis with a pair of olives. I was allowed two Roy Rogers with double cherries.

I never developed a taste for Scotch, my father's evening beverage of choice, although I must have mixed thousands of them for him in my childhood; I did however develop a fondness for gin, and I smoked Camels for a long time. One of the few possessions of my father's that I still have is the old marble ashtray that sat next to his chair in our house. For years, every time I stubbed out a cigarette in that ashtray, or let one burn all the way down to ash, I thought of him sitting in his chair drinking Scotch, smoking, and reading the

159

newspaper. I loved the image, cherished it. That ashtray connected us. I used to think, this ashtray killed my father, weakened his lungs, and now it's killing me. Finally I did the only prudent thing—I gave up cigarettes and retired the ashtray from active duty to a purely ornamental role.

My father died at home on the morning of my sixteenth birthday. He was fifty-six years old. He had been very ill with pneumonia, and in one of those haunting ironies had checked himself out of the hospital the day before against his doctor's advice so that he might be home for my birthday. It was the mistake of his life.

Exactly eleven days earlier my mother had died at age forty-five in a sanitarium in Lausanne, Switzerland. She had been in and out of institutions for fifteen years, waging a losing battle against chronic alcoholism. This was in the days before alcohol abuse, as it is now euphemistically known, had become fashionable, even heroic; the days when it was still stigmatized and shrouded in primitive misconception. In those days my mother was simply considered to be a hopeless drunk. On the day he told me of her death my father gave the cause as cirrhosis of the liver, under the circumstances an entirely plausible explanation. Not until a chance encounter with an old friend of my mother's on a city street several years ago did I learn the truth, that she had leapt to her death from a seventh-floor window. "Your mother was very brave," said the woman on the street, as a cold winter wind swirled off Lake Michigan.

My father shuffled into my room at five A.M. on the last morning of his life. We had buried my mother's ashes only a few days before. A few days later, when we buried my father, the earth would still be fresh on her grave, the flowers not even wilted. Between them lay the bones of their firstborn son, killed in an accident when he was just six years old. He was the joy of their life, and his death had broken their hearts so that they never again mended. Though it would take nearly twenty excruciating years, the guilt, the recriminations, and the despair, fueled of course by alcohol, had finally finished them both off.

My father's breath came hard and rasping. He needed me to call the doctor. Like all teenagers when awakened before dawn, I was cranky, annoyed at my father for disturbing me. I wanted to sleep late. It was spring vacation. It was my birthday. I got up slowly and grudgingly. Of course, I couldn't know that he was dying, but I will carry the shame of this behavior to my own grave. I remember it all so clearly.

The doctor didn't come in time. It was too early in the morning for him as well; he, too, was cranky and said to call back if my father got worse. I phoned three times before he finally agreed to come. He was too late. Nor did the ambulance arrive quickly enough. I should have called them sooner, but my father wanted the doctor. I did not know. My father's lungs filled with fluid and he drowned in his bed, before help arrived. I could do nothing but watch in horror as his face turned red and then a ghastly, terrifying purple. I hope I never see a face that color again. His body convulsed and then relaxed. I could do nothing but scream our address in the telephone to the ambulance dispatcher.

Later the negligent doctor (himself a drunk who would drop dead of a heart attack at a medical convention some years later—thus, as if in a preview of hell, attended in his own hour of need by all the physicians he could want) put a hand on my shoulder and told me that I was the man of the family now. What family? I asked.

There had been a family once, a family of three, now resting together at last. It began as a romantic story, the stuff of which cheesy television miniseries are made. My mother was a lovely French girl of aristocratic background who had married my father against her parents' wishes when she was just seventeen years old. He was a farm boy from Zanesville, Ohio, of strict Methodist upbringing, very much her social inferior, but eleven years older, a dashing army lieutenant and world-class polo player when they met, a man who many remarked bore more than a passing resemblance to Humphrey Bogart. "Wild Bill" Fergus, they called him in newspaper accounts of his polo exploits. In his riding breeches and boots, he cut quite a figure, though he had to rely on wealthy patrons for his mounts, and no others of the circle in which he and my mother met would become car dealers.

I am just the age now that my father was when I was born. He was forty, somewhat old, especially in those days, to be a new father. By then he was thoroughly addicted to Camels and sedated every evening by Dewar's. He was, in my memories at least, a sad, quiet man, for whom the light of life had already been extinguished, though I had no way of understanding that until many years after his death. He was strict, and like his father before him devoutly Republican, fair and decent, a fine, honorable man. I loved and respected him, and was a bit scared of him. I never saw him noticeably drunk, although he too was almost certainly an alcoholic. To be sure, theirs was a whole generation of boozers, our parents, giving birth to our own generation of whiners.

My parents never resolved the unspeakable question of which of them was responsible for their son's death. The bilious poison bubbled up frequently throughout my childhood. "You killed Billy!" my mother would shriek late at night, in a kind of insane alcoholic refrain which would finally drive my father from the house and down to the neighborhood bar, where he would anoint his own guilt with Scotch. Before she passed out, my mother, too drunk to walk, sometimes crawled on her hands and knees into my room. She would crawl to the edge of the bed and look in my face, so irredeemably drunk that she mistook me, a terrified ten-year-old, for my father. "Why don't you ever fuck me anymore?" she wanted to know. I pretended to be asleep, my eyes squeezed shut but leaking tears. I'd heard the question before. My father always answered without pity: "Go look in the mirror." I looked forward to the day when I might protect myself by saying hard things like that, and indeed, after I grew up I sometimes mistook myself for my father.

My parents were young and happy and in love once. I am greatly consoled by that knowledge; I have letters and photographs to prove it. They lived on a farm after the war, and Billy, their first-born son was a gorgeous child, apple of their eye. I have a photo of him on my desk. I look at it every day. I'm looking at it now. The photo was taken while my father was away during the war and my mother and Billy lived in New York. He is sitting on the edge of the fountain at the Plaza Hotel. He must be about five years old, only a year or so left in his short life. He wears a sweater, short pants, white socks folded down at the ankles, and shoes with straps. He has blond hair, a broad intelligent forehead, and large limpid eyes. With one hand he holds the thick chain that runs around the fountain, and he is looking at something off to the side. What is arresting about the photograph is the expression on his face. I have seen it in other pictures of him as well, an expression far too tragic, too knowing for a five-year-old. This is not hindsight on my part, but clearly premonition on his: Old before his years, that little boy knows something, some terrible secret thankfully hidden to the rest of us. In that little boy's eyes is not only his own death, but the rubble of his parents' lives as well, the sorrow. It is all there in this one photograph.

Billy was playing in a shed on the farm with a little girl named Kathy, the daughter of my parents' best friends. The tractor was parked in the shed, and the key was in the ignition. They started it. It was in gear, in reverse, and it lurched backward and Billy fell off and was pinned under the tire. His chest was crushed, though he lived for four agonizing hours. It was early in the morning, and my father and mother were both in the house when Kathy came in to report the accident. They ran out to the shed. I have this letter from my father's sister, dated August 3, 1947, describing what happened next: "Bill picked him up," my aunt wrote. "He said, 'Daddy, I'm hurt awful bad,' and started to cry. Bill said, 'Don't cry Billy,' and he stopped and never cried again. Bill carried him into their bed, the doctor came in ten minutes, and he was taken in ambulance to the hospital in Libertyville, and placed in an oxygen tent. He asked the nurse for ginger ale, and when she gave it to him he said, 'Thank you very much.' He kept saying over and over, 'Gosh, it hurts,' and then he would say, 'Run, Kathy, run,' and he called for Kathy and Jeffrey and told them to come play with him. And the last thing he did was he clicked at his pony to make him go faster, and Bill said an immortal thing. He said, 'Billy rode Peppy right up to heaven.' "

My father sat up all night by the open casket with the body of his son. The house was filled with flowers, so many flowers that they had to move most of the furniture down to the basement to accommodate them. I know what my father did there all night, I know what he thought, because, of course, sons are their fathers; I know it just as certainly as if I were sitting there myself. He smoked and he drank and he whispered to his son, he made him promises he would keep nineteen years later. And he wept. At four A.M., he went for a walk by himself, but not without first asking his sister to sit with Billy. He could not bear to leave his little boy alone in death. Already my parents were estranged—"somewhat at odds," my aunt tactfully put it in her letter—my mother sedated with morphine and, on the day of the funeral, numbed by sleeping pills. "It was the hottest day of the summer, that day," my aunt wrote in her letter over forty years ago, and still it brings the suffocating scent to my nostrils, "98 in the shade, and the smell of the flowers in the house was overpowering."

As I grew up, my parents never talked much about Billy, not while sober at least. I knew him only as a photograph in our living room, a sad-eyed, angelic-looking little boy in a white sailor suit, a ghost in the background of our lives. I never really even thought of him as my brother. How could I? In fact, only last year did I learn from my aunt's newly discovered letters that my parents had never intended to have any more children after Billy. My mother had not enjoyed the role of motherhood and had been inattentive to him, my father serving as both father and mother. "Bill clung to me," wrote my aunt of the day of Billy's death, "and said, 'Sis, everything in the world is wiped out for me.' Marie is hysterical, remorseful because she had not been a better mother, and she wants more children now." So in remorse and guilt and hysteria were my sister and I conceived in our mother's mind on that day.

My sister was born the following year, but still they wanted a son, and so I came into the world two years later. It is strange to learn now at my age that had Billy not died, I would never have existed. I don't know quite what to do with that information; it is an impossible responsibility. Billy's ghost continues to haunt me in ways I only begin to understand. My father was a good man, but everything in the world really was wiped out for him that day; and from then on, though he tried very hard, his heart wasn't in it, he was just marking time.

I will never have children of my own. A conscious choice, to break that particular chain. This world is no place for children. My father's pain is already more than I can bear; I inherited it in my genes as surely as I inherited his addictions, and it's so much harder to quit. I wish his son was still on earth. I wish I could go back, like in the movies, back in time to the morning of July 27, 1947. I want to go back and run in that shed and scream, "Don't turn that key, little boy!" Then I would sweep Billy off the tractor seat into my arms and carry him back as a gift to my father. To his father.

WHY I'M NOT A BANKER

by Robert F. Jones

The Stoats were one of the wealthier families in the Milwaukee of my youth, during and just after World War II. They may still be, for all I know or care. Back then in that town, money—I mean real money, with depth and resonance through local history—sprang from three major sources. There was brewing money, of course (the Pabsts, the Uihleins, who owned Schlitz, the Millers, et al.), manufacturing money (associated with such metal-eating firms as Allen-Bradley, A. O. Smith, Allis-Chalmers, and Evinrude), and the quietest yet most powerful of all, banking money. The Stoats were bankers, and my father worked for one of them: Morison Stoat, whom I disliked with ever increasing intensity.

He was a short, narrow-chested man, usually impeccably clad in subdued, pin-striped, double-breasted suits imported from some Eastern tailor—New York or Boston, probably the latter since Stoat had gone to Harvard and affected what to me sounded like a sissified Boston accent—through which a conspicuous potbelly poked despite that tailor's best efforts. Ruddy-faced with white, wavy hair and the thinnest wisp of close-trimmed hair on his upper lip that could still pass for a mustache, he had a long, I suppose you could say "patrician" nose, over which crawled a webwork of ruptured capillaries, like so many wireworms: the scars and portent of his affection for the bottle. In a town of brandy, bourbon, and beer drinkers, he drank Scotch—Black Label, of course. I didn't really dislike him for his looks, though, nor for the fact that once, while in his cups at a bankers' convention in Chicago, he had made a slobbering pass at my mother in a taxicab on Lincoln Drive, then passed out and (in her words) "wet his pants," ruining a skirt of hers in the process. After all, my mother was good-looking and boys will be boys. No, what I really resented, disliked—*despised*—in Morison Stoat was the fact that my father deferred to him.

It wasn't a flagrant deference, not of the grinning, yessing, ass-kissing, "oh-let-me-light-your-cigarette-and-pour-you-another-drink" variety no real man could stomach. It was more that my father took orders. Looking back, I suppose he had no choice. He was an ambitious, rising young officer in the bank, a tall, grave, deliberate man with no sense of romance and little of humor. He'd grown up poor, as he often told us, and his proudest boyhood memories were of scavenging the streets of Milwaukee for "horse apples," which he collected in a makeshift wagon and peddled to neighborhood gardeners for a nickel a load. He shoveled snow, mowed lawns, delivered papers, and in the summer "turned stile" at the ballpark, Borchert Field, in return for free admission during the final innings. Milwaukee was a much more Germanic town then than now, and when he saw a banner headline in the *Journal* one April day in 1917 (he would have been twelve years old at the time) saying AMERICA ENTERS WAR, he was mildly surprised to learn that we were going in on the side of the Allies. But the war created jobs for the young and undraftable. He soon quit school and went to work as a messenger boy at the bank, which had been owned since the Civil War by the Stoat family.

Somewhere about that time, in the public libraries he frequented, he discovered the Horatio Alger novels, and with them a blueprint for success: Poor lad rises to fame and fortune by hard work, clean living, self-improvement, and pinching his pennies so hard that Lincoln yells "Ouch!" He wasn't much fun as a dad, but he rose finally to become executive vice-president of the bank, despite what I still consider a valiant effort on my part to prevent it.

In the late 1940s we spent my father's two-week summer vaca-
tions on one or another of a chain of lakes in northern Wisconsin—
or "Up North," as we called it. The cottages we rented were small
and flimsily built, with no electricity and only a wood stove to take
the chill off the crisp Northern evenings. We fetched our water from a
squeaky, cast-iron hand pump—tan, ice-cold water that tasted
sharply of iron. The "bathroom" inevitably was a rickety, mal-
odorous two-holer out back, patrolled by vicious horseflies and
mosquitoes, and sometimes pine snakes that set my mother and
sister to shrieking. We lived largely on the fish we caught from the
lakes or the short connecting rivers that flowed between them.

I loved it Up North. I loved the heavy, leaky wooden rowboats
with an old coffee can for a bailer; the rickety piers that leaned out
into the lake with clouds of perch and bluegills circulating in and out
of their shadows; the pine snakes sinuating through the shallow
water, or up on the rocks, swallowing leopard frogs. Ospreys rowed
the air over the lake, rakish birds with fierce eyes who dove like
fighter planes to strafe the water and hook up a wriggling fish. And
each lake, it seemed in those days, had its family of loons—weird,
beautifully marked, low-swimming birds that dove deep and swam
far, then reemerged in the dusk of dawn or sunset to make the lake
echo with their eerie cowboy yodeling and wobbly laughter, the
essence of Up North.

There were loons on Balsam Lake, where we came one summer—
it must have been 1949, when I was fifteen. They were congregated,
probably nesting, at the north end of the long, narrow, rock-shored
lake where a gigantic lodge built of peeled, varnished white-pine logs
stood, in a big, square clearing now planted in neatly mowed blue-
green lawn. A long white dock projected into the lake from the
bottom of the lawn, with a white boat house squatting solidly beside
it. Now and then the boat house doors opened and a speedboat
emerged—a long, low, mahogany-hulled Chris Craft with a reverse
sheer to its cambered, drooping bow. A fast, rich boat with a powerful, throaty voice that sounded of money. It came out on weekends
to troll squealing young ladies and their shiny-toothed beaux behind
it, at creamy speed, on water skis. It raced the lake like it owned it, a

bone in its teeth, rocking the shores with its thunder and the rowdy waves raised by its wake. It ruined the fishing.

"Who owns that big place up there?" I asked my dad one morning. "Whose speedboat is that?"

"Stoat's," he said. "The family's had the place for years—built it back in the days of the lumber barons. I'm going up there this afternoon for a drink with Morison. Want to come along? Maybe he'll give us a ride on the boat."

I looked up the lake at Stoat's big place, then at the dinky cabin we rented.

"I wanted to fish this afternoon," I said. "There's been a hatch coming off the Lower River about four, four-thirty and I tied up some flies this morning that I think will match it. The trout jump all over that hatch."

"It'll be there tomorrow, won't it?"

"Maybe not," I said. "Who knows with hatches? Who knows with trout?"

My dad looked up the lake to where the American flag—a huge one—was snapping at the top of a tall white pole above Stoat's place.

"Pike are always in the same place," he said, distractedly. "And they're always hungry." He swatted at a deerfly that was buzzing his head. "Okay, but why don't you row me up there in the boat, then you can fish while I talk with Morison. You can have the boat."

"Is Mom going?"

"No," he said. "She doesn't feel well. Says she feels a headache coming on."

I thought, How can you feel a headache coming on? Either your head aches or it doesn't. Then I thought, Maybe she's more sensitive than I am.

I rowed my dad up there about three o'clock. Looking back over my shoulder to check my bearings, Stoat's place got bigger and bigger. It was a mansion. I could hear music from a Victrola echoing tinnily out over the water, someone singing some arty shit, probably opera. The speedboat was tied up to the neat, white dock, bumping languidly to the chop against neat, white fenders. Stoat came down the lawn to meet my father. He was wearing plaid Bermuda shorts and a fancy white shirt, all pleats and embroidery, that he called a Guayabera shirt, the hot item of late down Mexico way. His pale, skinny legs stuck out of the bottoms of the Bermudas like pipe cleaners, and he carried a big glass of Scotch in one hand, one of those double-walled plastic glasses that have fake trout flies embedded in them.

"You remember Bobby?" my dad said.

Stoat nodded and looked at me—looked *up* at me. I was taller than he was now. His eyes were a delicate blue, rimmed with a faint trace of biliousness in the whites, and thinner, fainter cousins of the wireworms on his nose. Shrewd eyes, chilly, giving away nothing but quick to read weaknesses. A gunfighter's eyes, or a poker player's.

"He's grown," Stoat said. "That's some tan he's got, Chahley, black as a Nigro."

I looked down into the speedboat—leather seats, gleaming brightwork, rich, clear-lacquered mahogany strakes. Mooring lines faked down to perfection. Out on the lake a loon was sounding off. *Ha-oo-oo. Ha-ooo-oo-oo . . .*

"Gawd damn those birds," Stoat said, petulant. "They wake me up every morning with that dratted laughter." But he said it more like "drotted loffter."

They walked up toward the lodge, my dad swinging along in his giraffelike stride, Stoat a full head or more shorter than he. On the screened-in porch I could see the glint of tines on the big-racked deer heads mounted there.

I rowed down to the far end of the lake, enjoying the sun and the heavy swing of the oars, the stretch and pull of my back muscles. Two loons followed along with me, swimming about thirty or forty yards ahead or abeam of the boat, diving occasionally and reemerging like checker-backed corks at impossible distances from their points of submersion. I could see the flies coming off the Lower River as I neared it—big gray drakes that took a long time getting off the water—and the heavy rise-rings of trout feeding on them as they emerged.

I fished them for an hour, catching one trout after another, mainly brookies but a few big sullen browns mixed in there with them, their black spots big as dimes against the old gold when I netted them. I was wading barefoot in my shorts, a flybox rolled up in the sleeve of my T-shirt like a cigarette pack, the net and the live-stringer looped on my belt. Now and then the stringer's twitching load would foul the net and I'd stop to clear it and maybe pluck a few bloodsuckers off my legs—the lake was alive with leeches—but mainly I fished hard. Then, when the sun was sloping low, fattening and reddening, I heard the boom of the first gunshot.

The speedboat was coming down the lake with Stoat at the wheel, idling along at half speed, and I could see my dad standing up on the engine coaming with a shotgun. He was watching the water intently. Then he raised the gun suddenly—it was a long-barreled pump— and fired abeam. I saw the shot pattern slash the water, long and ragged and white, and a black head disappear near it. Stoat spun the wheel and hit the throttle and the speedboat went from a burble to a roar, heading in the direction of where the shot hit. They circled the spot, staring down at the water. Stoat's voice came faint and querulous over the water, "You missed the bahstahd, Chahley!"

They were shooting at loons.

I climbed in the rowboat, took down the rod, cased it, and sat there waiting as the speedboat hunted its way toward me. I was shivering, not entirely from the cold water or the breeze that was kicking up with sunset.

"Morison's going to tow us back to the cottage," my dad said when they pulled alongside. "Come on, get in and dry off."

"I'll stay in the rowboat," I said. "It'll need some weight aft to keep from taking water over the bow."

"Suit yourself." He could see I was pissed and I saw his face stiffen. But when I swung the stringer into the boat he whistled. "You did all right," he said.

I only grunted.

"Hand that stringer up here," my dad said. "We've got ice aboard."

I handed him the stringer. Stoat was sipping Scotch from one of his fancy glasses. He looked at the fish as they swung aboard and raised his eyebrows in mock surprise. "For me?" he said with a tight little grin. "Why, thank you, Bobby."

Back on our own pier we watched Stoat race up the lake, throwing huge waves as he went.

"It's illegal to shoot loons," I said.

"Morison was too drunk to shoot," my father said.

"But it's illegal."

"Cripes O'Grady," he said, shaking his head and not looking at me. "They were keeping him up at night, waking him up in the morning."

"It's still illegal."

"What're you going to do? Turn him in to the game warden? Turn *me* in? He owns this whole lake, this cottage, all these places. He owns half the county, maybe more. You don't understand yet. There are certain things you have to do when a man's your boss."

"You didn't have to give him all the trout."

"We've got a steak for dinner," he said, slapping me on the back. "Anyway, you'll catch more."

I lay awake late that night, up in the sleeping loft, plotting revenge. There was an auger in one of the drawers downstairs. I was good in the water, already a state champion on the high school swim team. I could sneak up to Stoat's one night—tonight, in fact—and hole his speedboat below the waterline. Wait, even better—I could drill a hole in the bottom, plug it with a cork from, say, a whiskey bottle (ah, yes, a little irony in that touch), attach a long line from the cork to the dock, underwater. Then the next time Stoat took it out on the lake . . . Beautiful! I could see it all unfold—him revving up the boat, casting off his lines, then roaring away from the dock, Scotch in hand, to the end of the tether (my dad's fishing line, off his Plueger, would do very nicely), and then, pop! Like a cork from a champagne bottle. A christening in reverse.

"What are you laughing at up there?" my dad asked from the foot of the ladder.

"Nothing," after a long, sullen pause.

He was quiet for a minute, then I heard him coming up the ladder. He sat next to me in the dark.

"You're still angry about the loons."

"Not really."

He put his hand on my shoulder, there in the dark.

"Well, I'm sick about it," he said.

"It's all right," I said.

"No it's not. It's rotten." He took his hand away. "I tried to shoot over them at first, but he just kept watching for them to pop up, kept running over within range."

"You could quit the bank," I said.

He laughed, once, a short, hard snort. "And do what for a living?"

"I was planning how to sink his speedboat," I said.

"You wouldn't want to do that!" He sounded really shocked.

"The hell I wouldn't."

He was silent for a while. Then he stood up. "I wish you wouldn't use bad language," he said.

In the morning I waded the shoreline with the flyrod, throwing a bassbug at the rise-rings in the lily pads. No wind. Dead quiet. You could hear the plop of the rising bass, feeding, and the distant smack of my dad's axe on pine billets. I found two loons dead on the sand, washed up by the night wind. What looked like another one was snagged, belly up, in the weedbed offshore.

Someone walked out on the lawn at Stoat's place, a servant no doubt, and raised the American flag. I threw it a loose salute: clenched fist, erect middle finger. Then I threw the dead loons back into the woods, food for the foxes and ravens.

INTO THE CUT

by Robert Olmstead

Between Lost Swamp and Ossabaw Sound the Ogeechee River hooks, bends, and turns on itself, bulging with six-hour tides that flood the marshes and timber swamps. It's here the Georgia razorback proliferates, living off grasses, tubers, frogs, the young of rabbits, cottonmouths, and an occasional fawn. Growing out of their jaws are sets of tusks and sharpeners that work like knife and steel. Their hides are a thick shell of muscle and gristle and it's needed because the hog's second most favorite thing to do is fight.

Dewey and Ron stand at the fire barrel, treading in place to keep warm, waiting for Payton to get in from Texas. Hanging behind them are hooks, gambrels, and spreaders. Hides too: coon, beaver, and fox. In back are the dogs, hunting dogs, and all around the camp, swamp and yellow slash pine rise a hundred feet into the gray sky, some giving way to the ice, going off like rifle shots, trunks exploding in the freezing air. It's South Georgia, January, wet, and 27 degrees.

Ron asks Dewey if he heard the joke about the boy who fell in love with a mule. Dewey says no, and Ron's disappointed, as if Dewey might've been the one who could tell him a joke he's heard about, but hasn't heard.

Payton pulls up in his truck. He slides out the door and in the same motion ascends the sideboards and begins handing down chain saws, a battery, and gas cans.

Dewey and Ron lift the dog box and slide it onto the bed.

175

"Your daddy kill hisself yet?" Ron yells.

"Not yet," Payton says. "But he plans to sometime this afternoon. Get them dogs up here. Now."

Dewey and Ron go out behind the shed and come back with two dogs.

"This one right cheer is Rambo," Ron says, hoisting up a black and tan. "He's bout as ugly too, but he's a ground-burnin' sum bitch and he's been known to find lost dogs."

Dewey brings on Snowball, a husky shepherd mix with one blue eye. They latch the doors, then swing the boat trailer onto the ball and cuff it down.

"You find that High Low dog or your daddy gonna kill hisself, you hear? He's your daddy's best boar dog. Without that High Low dog, he say, he won't hunt no mo hog."

Payton looks down at him and then to Dewey. Dewey don't ever say nothin'. He's always black with soot from woodsmoke. He lives in a schoolbus, burns an open fire, and wears other people's clothes. He don't care so much as Ron does. Ron was in the National Guard. Both men work for Payton's father, running trapline, a hundred miles in South Carolina alone. They guide too. Hunters come for whitetail that live off the mast of live oak and beech and browse the young pine. Or the hunters come for boar hog.

"Gas in there for that motor?" Payton asks, nodding his head toward the boat.

"She's full. You just find that High Low dog or your daddy gone to kill hisself."

Payton gets in his truck and rolls down the window. He adjusts the mirrors, then lights a smoke.

"Either way, says he gone to do it," Payton says. "Sometime after lunch. You go on up. Might let you watch."

"Well, I hope your momma's got sense enough to call down here if he does. Me and Dewey will want to know."

Payton shakes his head and starts the engine. He pulls around the circle and in his rear-view sees them hovering at the fire barrel again, beaver castors and spoonlike baculums hanging from the beam over their heads. Somewhere farther back a tree trunk goes off, ripping open the morning like the sound of double-ought buck from a poacher's gun. Dewey and Ron duck their heads at the sounds as if sound could hurt them.

Three days ago, Payton was running an irrigation crew out of Jim Hogg County, Texas, a crew of wets who had a tendency to kill each other. His daddy called to say he'd just made a lot of money ferrying movie crews in and out of the marsh. They built a POW camp and Ron and Dewey got parts as dead men. It was a Vietnam movie, one where the hero goes back years later to free his buddies. He told Payton about the lost High Low dog and said only Payton could find him, said he'd kill himself if Payton didn't. Payton told him he might's well load the gun, hung up the phone and packed his bag.

Lance is standing by his mailbox when Payton comes by. Rambo and Snowball start a racket in the back, yipping and growling at him. Lance cusses them out, tells them to shut their G.D. mouths, then cusses the cold.

"Your daddy kill hisself yet?"

"Kiss my ass," Payton says, "and get yours in this here truck."

They jounce along the back roads making for the boat landing. Lance goes into his coat pockets and comes out with a paperback and a pint of Evan Williams. He reads and sips as he rides. He doesn't do much else in life but nurse what's left of his inheritance, money his granddaddy made bagging up sugar sweepings from boxcars and selling it to moonshiners.

For years he's watched Payton and his father war with each other. Five months ago when Payton dusted for Texas he was a little sad to lose his friend, a little sad the fighting could be over.

It starts to snow again. Payton turns on the wipers, but the one on Lance's side just lays there. Lance looks up from his book.

"You see Leann since you got back? She's five months gone. Says it's yours."

The dogs start another ruckus in the back. Payton pounds the rear window and tells them to quiet down or he'll shoot them, then he gets his hands back on the wheel.

"What she is and what she says is two different things."

He says it in a way that lets Lance know it's something to keep shut up about.

They ride in silence the rest of the way to Richmond Hill where they launch the boat on the high tide. Payton parks the truck and takes his .44 from under the seat. When his daddy gave it to him he said, This here gun packs a world of killing. They're words he's never forgotten.

The water's rough and the snow is now rain. They hunker down on their seats, the dogs between their legs among buckets, lines, muzzles, and cushions as they make the run across the Ogeechee.

It's fifteen minutes before the thudding chop against the steel hull diminishes and they leave the river for the Cut. Here begins a web of canals, Peachtree, Valambrosia, Elbow, Walker, Red Dock, and New Hope. All dug by slaves to make rice paddies now grown over with marsh grass and cattails.

The rain has stopped but they're wet; a stiff wind blows and the sky is ash white. From the northwest comes the sound of thunder, Fort Stewart practicing artillery.

"Bow, Rambo. Bow, Snowball," Payton yells. "Hunt 'em up 'bo. Hunt 'em up. Find that High Low dog."

The two dogs crowd the bow, their noses sorting out what rides the wind. These dogs live to hunt wild boar and about five are lost every year in that pursuit, if not to boar, then to gators or cottonmouth. Payton knows it's the way it goes, but not for the High Low dog. That old boy was made to hunt boar hog. Payton's daddy raised him from a pup, raised him up to be a boar-hunting machine. Without that High Low dog, Payton's daddy won't ever go into the marsh again.

Inside the Cut, marsh grasses are bent and each one is encased in ice. Jagged plates of it have formed at the banks and pockets of mist rise up around them.

Rambo and Snowball hover at the bow, their backs a sheen of frozen spray. Even with the motor running, everything is quiet and still. They ride the canals all morning, setting out the dogs and Payton following them into the marsh while Lance stays with the boat, circling around if he can and picking them up on the other side, sometimes a half mile away. They're soaked to the bone in a rising wind and the throb of dull pain echoes through their limbs to their guts with every move they make.

A redtail hawk scissors the air and Payton points out a palm tree on a levee where one summer a copperhead bit him. He tells Lance about the night he was coon hunting on the river. The stick broke and before he could shut down the motor he hit a log and capsized. He dove in to cut his dogs free, slicing his own hand to the tune of thirty-seven stitches. Two dogs drowned that night.

"After all these years runnin' with you," Lance says, "I don't like you much, but I do enjoy you."

As he says this, Rambo and Snowball leap from the bow into the water, baying up a boar hog nesting at the edge. Lance runs the boat aground and they follow through the swamp trying to get in on it, but breaking out on the far side is another canal and by the time they bust through, the hog's in the water and the dogs are onto its black bullet of a head.

Payton jumps in grabbing the boar by its ears and dragging it to shore. It goes under and he goes with it, but when he comes up he's alone. They collar the dogs and wait, but it's no use. The boar's sunk in the cold water and is drifting to the sea. Steam billows from them as the air takes their body heat. They stand waist deep in near frozen water, yet it feels warm and there's still no sign of the High Low dog, dead or alive.

"It's noon," Lance says. "We go back now we might get warm and get to see yo daddy kill hisself."

Payton's jaw is so tight with cold he thinks it might shatter into little pieces of bone that'd tinkle down through his body.

"I'll hold these dogs. You fetch that boat round to this here point, Mr. Downtown Lance. When I was in Texas I learned there was more ways to kill a man than I already knew and right now, you don't get that boat, your livin' is what's gone to kill you."

Lance disappears in the marsh grass and Payton waits huddled with the dogs. He thinks how overnight his father has gone from being a mean man to being a weak man and it leaves him with an anger boiled down from old rage. If he finds the High Low dog, his daddy will get mean again and if he doesn't he'll kill himself. He'll show them all he's still got it in him to at least do something right. It hurts to smile, but Payton does, knowing either way, things will work out for the best.

Lance motors around to the point. He's got a fire going inside an old tar bucket. It's smoky but warm and Payton gets over it letting the fumes bathe his chest, neck, and face.

"How them dogs gone to smell anything with this stinkpot," he says, coughing out his words.

"You racin' your daddy to hell?"

"Wouldn't be no race to watch, I'll tell you that," Payton says.

Lance cranks the stick and the boat moves forward. They ride slowly, swinging near the bank to collect sticks of wood for the bucket. Payton lets the dogs get warm, then sends them to the bow. Away from the heat and smoke they get doglike again, dancing and skittering, craning their necks and sniffing the air.

"Some say that baby in Leann was made by one of them stuntmen boys from the movie. Little man who took the fall every time one of them Veet Nameese was shot."

"Had enough of this," Payton says and his hands sizzle as he claps them around the fire bucket, picks it up, and casts it over the side. The dogs pivot to see what bangs in the water. They don't look to Payton to see where it comes from, they only look to where the sound was and he likes that.

"Hunt 'em up, 'bo," he yells. "Hunt 'em up. Git that High Low dog. Snatch him from the jaws of death."

Rambo kees and yips while Snowball stares forward, her good eye blue as slate and the other milky white. They pass under an osprey nest and the dogs explode from the bow, beating the air for land. It's a two-hundred-pound black boar hog and he's madder than hell. He has no intention of drowning. He tries to break for it, but Rambo gets an ear and Snowball clamps onto his hind end. The three of them tumble to the ground.

The boar comes up fighting. As he gets one dog down the other jumps him. More than anything he wants to sink a tusk into Snowball's soft belly and lay it open to her neck, but neither dog backs off. Sheets of marsh grass fall under them while mud and water fan the air.

Payton and Lance follow behind, trying to get in tight, sometimes knee deep in the rising tide. Lance grabs Rambo by the tail and drags him off. The dog has lost an ear and blood wells from its head. Payton gets between Snowball and the boar, then raises the .44. The hog comes on and he fires, dropping it at his feet.

It all happens at once, and it's in this moment that Payton lives his life. He knows it and it's like memory to him, something not learned, only forgotten, an imprint for some that's faded from what used to be to what's become. There's five of them on that island, ranging from dead to alive.

"Weren't no call to shoot that hog," Lance says quietly. "You don't need no meat. We coulda got off safe."

"It's finished," Payton says pointing the .44 to a mound back through an alley in the marsh.

Lance can see what's left of a half-eaten dog strewn at the base of it. He looks back at the hog, goes down on a knee in the mud.

"Them eyes," he says, "I never thought it before, but dead or alive they look the same."

Payton takes off his jacket and hands it to Lance. Then he takes off his shirt and goes to Snowball. She stands shivering, her intestines hanging in the water between her legs. Payton tucks them back in, trussing his shirt around her belly, then gets back inside his jacket.

Payton and Lance dock the boat, setting the dogs out to stand on the hardwood planks. The air is raw, and feels like rough hides dragged across your skin. Rambo drags a leg and Snowball's belly has frozen shut in Payton's shirt. When it thaws she'll drop her guts and die. The boar hog lays in the bow, his eyes still sharp as tungsten, and Lance stares at it, gut hot with hard liquor.

"Take that boat around," Payton says, stamping his feet to bring his legs some life.

Cradling Snowball in his arms, and with Rambo limping behind, he goes to the truck while Lance motors around to the landing. His daddy's truck is parked beside his with the engine running. When he gets near, his daddy and Leann get out and wait for him.

"You find that High Low dog?" his daddy says.

"Did you kill yo'self?" Payton says.

"No, but now I'm gone to, you didn't find that High Low dog."

Payton can see how Leann's belly has grown big inside her coat.

"That's mine," he says to her.

She nods and then she smiles, her face going pretty with relief. Payton smiles too and then looks to his father.

"Me and Lance," he says, "we hunted up that boar hog what ate the High Low dog. We shot that boar and cut him open and your High Low dog come jumping out and here he is daddy."

"You lie, boy, you lie to yo daddy. Yo daddy gone kill hisself tonight."

"That's right, daddy. I am a liar and if you're a fool you will make my momma a widow forever."

He holds the dog out to his father, thinking how hearts are just muscles to be made stronger. He depends on knowing this and on knowing his father will take hold of the dog, not letting it fall to the ground between them.

LAST RITES

by William Hjortsberg

My father died when I was eleven, six months after he moved his restaurant business from New York to Florida. He had a heart attack while driving down from Tampa and managed to stagger into a drugstore before collapsing in the phone booth. My mother insists he knew the end was coming and tried to call her with his last breath. But something about the tone of her voice makes me think she holds it against him for dying before he got his dime in the slot.

My father was cremated, according to his wishes. I remember sitting alone with Mother on a plush velvet couch in the crematorium. A somber gentleman with the manners of a headwaiter drew back the velour drapes in front of us, and we looked into an antiseptic white-tiled room. In the center stood my father's coffin, resting on a stainless-steel table and surrounded by showy banks of memorial flowers. The lid was closed now, and the mahogany sides shone with a luster as bright as my new cordovan shoes. A faint organ tremolo signaled the entrance of two workmen wearing khaki janitor's uniforms. They wheeled the table over to a vaultlike door in the end wall. My mother turned her face away, weeping. There wasn't much more to see; the iron door opened, and the workmen took hold of the brass handles and slid the coffin inside. The curtain silently closed. The show was over.

For the rest of the year, Mother kept my father's ashes in a number ten can in the hall closet. I knew it was there behind the galoshes.

When my mother was away for the day, I carried it out into the living room and tried to get the lid off. I was curious to know how they condensed my father—as well as that bulky, polished coffin—down into such a small can.

The lid was jammed on tight. I was afraid to go at it with a screwdriver for fear of leaving telltale scratches. Finally, I held the can under the hot-water tap in the bathtub. Twenty minutes of steam treatment. Back in the living room, I wrapped a towel around the lid for traction and tugged. The hot water did the trick. The lid came off easily, but I upset the can on the rug.

My father's remains spilled out across the living room floor. I sat horrified, while above my head a thick, white cloud of powdery ash hovered in the sunlight, precipitating gently onto the coffee table and couch. When terror passed, I dusted myself off and considered the situation. Things weren't so bad. I knew my mother was out for the afternoon and the door was locked against unexpected visitors. I decided to indulge my curiosity and began prodding through the ashes with a pencil like a sneezing Sherlock Holmes. A quantity of ticklish stuff had gotten up my nose.

I was looking for something solid, a brass coffin handle or dentures, anything that would equate what had come out of the furnace with what I had seen going in. But I found nothing substantial enough to suggest bone or coffin parts or the heavy Masonic ring I had never seen my father without—not even the morning of his funeral when it glittered on his folded, waxlike hands.

My father had been a work of art, a testimonial to the mortician's skill. "So lifelike," was the comment of Mrs. Friedman, our lawyer's wife. But he had been more than that, much more than lifelike; the shadows under his eyes had been eradicated along with the liver splotches on his cheeks, and his lips were rouged like a silent-movie actor's. My father's corpse was a flattering caricature of the man he had been in life.

Crafty fellows, those morticians. They restore the dead with the skill of taxidermists—nostrils plugged to prevent leakage, jaws wired shut to avoid the embarrassment of a yawning mouth during the funeral service—and they possess a fire intense enough to reduce even large chunks of metal to the consistency of chalk dust. But I'm on to them. I found them out fourteen years ago when I poked through my father's ashes with the pointed tip of a pencil.

Behind those impressive crematorium doors lurked hired underlings who wrenched my poor father from his coffin, stripped him of his jewelry and gold teeth, and tossed him naked into the fire. And the coffin, with the satin cushions smoothed out, was wheeled back to the showroom to be resold. How I longed to change my costume in the security of a secret cave and emerge as Batman or Straight Arrow to expose this gang.

The real problem was cleaning up the mess in the living room. No explaining would have helped. Not even uncovering the mortician's plot excused the desecration of my father's ashes. I scraped what I could back into the can but it was still half empty. Mother would have detected the difference in weight, so I filled it the rest of the way with a box of cake mix from the kitchen and tamped the lid firmly into place.

I was using the vacuum cleaner on the rug when the doorbell rang. Some well-meaning neighbor coming to offer belated condolences. "Just a minute," I called, clicking off the machine. I carried the can, now half Betty Crocker, back to its resting place in the closet. The frustrated buzzing continued. I swung open the front door. It was Scotty Sickler, a sixth-grade classmate.

"Hiya," Scotty said. "Whatcha been doing?"

"Nothing special," I said, blocking the door. "Look, Scotty, you can't come in right now."

"Why not?"

"Doctor's orders. The house is quarantined 'cause I've got the measles."

"Oh, that's okay then. I've already had the measles."

"Which kind?"

"Both kinds, German and regular. So it's okay, I'll come in and keep you company for a while."

Damn you, Scotty Sickler, I thought, you and your damn immunity to disease. If you found out about the living room, it'd be all over school by lunch period recess Monday morning. "No, I don't think you better, Scotty," I said, "what I've got is Turkish measles."

"The *Turkish* measles?"

"Yeah, it's different. See, no spots."

"Well, I never heard of any Turkish measles."

"It's very contagious," I said. "Right this minute you could be getting infected with it."

"Okay." Scotty backed away a few feet. "Are you sure it's the Turkish measles?"

"That's what the doctor said."

Scotty climbed on his bicycle.

I closed the door and leaned back against it. Scotty Sickler was a great fishing friend but no one to trust with a secret. In the living room, I discovered the cat had been in the ashes. His paw prints tracked through every room in the house. It took over an hour to vacuum up the last incriminating trace of my father.

The number ten can stayed in the hall closet until the end of summer when Mother sold the house and we returned to New York. We took a cruise ship from Miami. The second day out, my mother said she had something she wanted to talk about in the cabin.

"This is very serious, Benjy," she said, "and very sad. I couldn't say anything about it at mealtimes because of all the other people at the table. There are some things a family has to keep to itself." She sat next to me on the lower bunk and gripped my hand.

"You know, Benjy, when your father passed away, that was a sad time for both of us and I don't like to remind you. But you see, your father hasn't gone to his final resting place yet, Benjy. It was his desire to be buried at sea. He loved the water so much, always off fishing and never at home. It's fitting; it's where he wanted to be."

"Please, Mom, you're hurting my hand." Her fingernails left a painful row of indentations across the back of my hand.

"I didn't mean to hurt you, dear."

"It's all right."

"I've never hurt you, you know that. Never in your life have I hurt you."

"I never said you did, Mom."

"Don't ever tell me that I've hurt you."

"I won't, Mom." I took my mother's hand and gave it a big squeeze. "Honest, I won't."

"Oh, I know, Benjy. You're a good boy." She blew her nose into a Kleenex.

"What were you saying about Pop being buried at sea?" I felt silly about referring to a can of ashes and cake mix as "Pop."

Mother sniffled. "I have his ashes here on the boat. I couldn't say anything about it at the table the way those others are always snooping. Certain things are private. This morning I went to see the captain about a funeral. Something simple was all I wanted. 'Just the chaplain or yourself to say a few words,' I told him. It was my husband's last request; his oldest friend in the Merchant Marine was torpedoed during the war and went down with his ship. I was sure the captain would understand that. After all, he's a nautical man himself. But he said no. Something about regulations, he said. Can you believe it, Benjy—a little thing, a prayer for the dead, and he refused. What kind of regulations would stop a man from praying?" Mother shredded her Kleenex into her lap.

"Then we're not going to have a funeral? I mean, what are we going to do with Pop?" A spark of panic was touched off at this possibility, igniting the fear that my mother might have some more romantic plan in mind for the disposal of my father's ashes, like scattering them to the winds over New York City from an airplane. What would she say when the first handful turned out to be powdered angel food mix?

Mother dabbed at her eyes with a torn piece of tissue no bigger than a postage stamp. "We're going to have to take care of things ourselves, Benjy," she said. "We'll hold our own funeral; I'm sure your father wouldn't mind that. I've arranged with the florist on the promenade deck to send down a nice bouquet tomorrow morning. Then we'll find a quiet spot on deck and have a simple Christian service all by ourselves."

The next morning after breakfast, my mother and I made our appearance on A-Deck. We were dressed completely in black in spite of the September heat. I wore the woolen suit that had hung in my closet since the day of my father's cremation. Mother had on a veil. We walked single file, with slowly measured steps, down the entire length of the deck. In my arms I carried an immense basket of white roses, my father's favorite, while my mother carried Father himself— his little can all done up with the ribbons and a bow like a giftbox of chocolates.

We stood together by the rail at the stern, and while I dropped the roses, a blossom at a time, into the boiling wake, my mother read aloud from the "Order for the Burial of the Dead" in the *Book of Common Prayer*. I remember her reading the obsequies in a voice strong enough to carry over the noise of a shuffleboard game in progress behind us.

" 'Unto Almighty God we entrust the soul of our brother departed,' " Mother read, " 'and we commit his body to the deep.' " And with that she tumbled the beribboned can off the rail. I watched it fall, end over end, and saw it swallowed up soundlessly in the foam. Dozens of white roses, together with the floating peels of several hundred oranges, marked the spot where it went under the surface.

"Let us pray," my mother intoned, bowing her head. I folded my hands in a gesture of piety, but my thoughts were far away from Mother's mumbled prayers. I was thinking of my father's can on its final journey to the bottom of the sea. Even at that moment, the water was slowly seeping in, activating the cake mix as the can spiraled deeper and deeper. I thought of the mix foaming into a batter, forcing the lid and easing my father—in a sweet soufflé—out of the cruel confines of the can. All along the way, for fathoms and fathoms, schools of blue-water fish gathering to feed.

THE OTHER FORT WORTH BASSES

by Rick Bass

First off, he smokes Viceroy cigarettes. They keep him skinny, like a bullwhip. He's almost eighty-eight, and clear-eyed.

When Granddaddy was twenty-seven, he drove down from his home in Fort Worth into the Texas hill country, looking for some country to lease so he could deer hunt. He found the place he wanted by serendipity, or sixth sense, by just staying after it, wandering, looking, and all the while closing in on it. He found the place that would become his camp, and later my father's and uncle's camp, and my camp . . .

We call it the Deer Pasture, and it has become our family history. There are two creeks, which eventually flow into the Pedernales River. We regard water on the Deer Pasture as even more of a miracle than it usually is. In the hill country, where the summer days hit a hundred degrees, the blaze heat bouncing off all those boulders and canyons makes us, as well as the wildlife, prize the water in those creeks.

Great live oak trees line the creeks, and scrub cedars blanket the steep hills. Shy deer and turkeys step through the dark cedars; doves call. I've taken pictures along the creek of bobcats, foxes, coyotes, skunks, raccoons, quail, roadrunners, rattlesnakes, and a mountain lion. The Deer Pasture is a perfect mix of the rough (boulders,

189

cedars, cacti) and the pastoral (small meadows, ponds, shady oak trees along the creeks). I think our family of rough men has always aspired to that ideal mix of strength and finesse. Drawn to the Deer Pasture by Granddaddy sixty-four years ago, we chase that mix of nature every year in November, when all the men in the Bass family gather to hunt the first week of deer season. From wherever we're living, it's a tradition that we can count on, one we look forward to all year: Granddaddy, my father and my two brothers, my uncle and *his* three sons . . .

Our family works mostly with the earth for a living, and always has. I'm a geologist, my father's a geophysicist. Uncle Jimmy threads and sells drilling pipe, and Randy and Russell, his two youngest sons, help him run the business.

Where once all the Bass men were bull *ruffians,* there's hope for Bass men to come. We're learning. There *is* hope. Uncle Jimmy's oldest son (also named Rick) is, of all things, a gynecologist. And his specialty is difficult pregnancies—fertility. He specializes in getting women pregnant, is how we refer to it.

I grapple with the earth, as a geologist, but I also write, and my middle brother, Frank, is a journalist. Not that writing is as feminine as gynecology, but it's still a far cry from shoving drilling pipe down into the earth. My youngest brother, B.J., is still in high school. He doesn't play football, like Frank and I did. B.J. plays tennis.

There are two outcropping rock formations on the Deer Pasture. One of these represents the oldest rocks in the country: Precambrian sandstones that are over a billion years old. The other outcrop consists of young rocks, volcanic dikes and sills that pushed up through fractures in the ancient Precambrian rocks. These younger rocks, the granite especially, are not as enduring or resistant as the old sandstones. They're richer, though, because they crumble easily and release nutrients back into the soil. The granite boulders decompose into nuggets and gravels that we call "chat," which is a beautiful rose-pink color.

A hundred and fifty years ago, so say the old journals of the area, it was almost all grassland on the Deer Pasture. Then cattle moved in. Now it's woodland, with oaks and hickories and lovely smelling, dusky blue-berried cedar springing up on the flat mesas. Cedar swarms the land, and we try to keep it cut back. But it grows fast and tries to change the face of the land, tries to change things. And we want to keep some meadows and grassland open, the way it was. Granddaddy, Uncle Jimmy, and Daddy think it's silly that we boys work to keep the cedar out.

"Let it go," they say. "Just let it go."

But we want those soft green meadows: all that grass. We want to bring some of the meadows back.

I think we want a thing, in our rough way, without even knowing what that thing is. We feel a hunger for a thing we don't have. It's a dimmer instinct—almost an *animal* instinct—but that doesn't make it any less lovely.

Still, our genes for *enduring* persist. We'll always have that rough stuff, though, no matter how refined we may get. My grandfather gave it to my father, and my father gave it to me, and I know myself well enough that, despite my efforts to cultivate a more artistic side, I'm still going to have plenty to pass on to *my* son . . . or daughter . . .

There was a time, eight or so years ago, when Old Granddaddy was not so clear-eyed. He'd had a stroke at the age of eighty and we did not think he would make it another year. We thought that way for several years. Then he had surgery on the tendons in his wrists and hands, so that he could pull the trigger once more, and he learned to speak, once more. He got cornea implants that made his eyesight a perfect 20/20—better than any of ours. But he still smokes those cigarettes. He sits up in the granite boulders and, while hunting with the wind in his face, he inhales those damn Viceroys, which we won't let him into the lodge with because none of the rest of us smoke.

With the exception of Randy, who's a poet these days, and my father, who's becoming one, we're all hunters. Randy and my father prefer to watch the deer rather than hunt them. But Old Granddaddy is neither a hunter nor a poet. From the old school, he's simply a *shooter*. It's what he knows—hunting deer on this land—and it's all he's ever done.

There was a long dry spell, those years when we wondered if each year would be his last, when he didn't get a deer—when he couldn't even see a deer through the scope. Now it's like the old days. He shoots two deer a year (my father takes one home, and Randy takes the other) because that's the legal limit. It's also how Granddaddy is, and there's no need to try to change him, lecture, or judge him. If the limit were three deer a year instead of two, he'd shoot three. Not only do I not judge Granddaddy for being such an inveterate deerslayer, I am glad that he is. He gives our younger wanderings a dimension, a backdrop, and he gives us meat, too.

The severity of Granddaddy's sharp-eyed judgment, the harshness of sentence—the crack of his little rifle, a flat-shooting .222—contrasts nicely with the younger elements of the land. My brothers, Frank and B.J., or myself will sometimes go off deep into the woods with a book in the pocket of our baggy camouflage pants. We'll hunt a while, then read, then sit among those boulders and feel the sixty-four years we'll never know except through stories, and we'll think, sometimes, with courage, of the sixty-four years we *will* know, the years lying in front of us . . .

But our family's changing. The core of it's the same, but other parts of it, like the land, are changing, and it's a fine thing to see. Like in the evenings, when we sit around the fire and drink whiskey and talk about what each of us is doing, what has happened in the past year. We tell stories and listen, again and again, to the things that have happened to us in the past. We tell about the night the wild pigs chased Uncle Jimmy up the tree, and the time that old Jack, the camp cook, got blind drunk at lunch and picked up a pistol and shot a flying turkey.

We talk about *everything*. And we drink too much whiskey at night by the fire. We keep pulling back the past, pulling it back in as if it's attached to the end of a rope. Each year we sit around those campfires and strain to pull it all the way back in, like a bucket at the bottom of a well. Our intentions are to pull it in close enough to reach it, touch it, inspect it, *feel* it: to make sure it's all still in good shape and that none of it's missing.

My father's fifty-eight. I'm thirty-four. Soon it will be time for me to make my parents be grandparents . . .

My father tends to Granddaddy—Old Granddaddy. He pampers him, helps him hike all over the rough country, lifts and cleans and carries his kills in to the lodge. He fixes Granddaddy's favorite meals—ham and biscuits with grits and red-eye gravy. Granddaddy eats them with a vengeance—leaning over the plate and shoveling the food in, eyes watering with the spice and pleasure of it. And when Granddaddy's done and satisfied, my father brings him his drink.

Granddaddy usually crawls into his bunk around midnight. The rest of us stay out at the fire until two or so. Russell, my youngest cousin at twenty-nine, goes through his usual phase of mixed melancholia and pride, sounding as if *he* is a grandfather. What he does is enumerate his company's successes until Randy, who's been looking east, looking out at the stars, looking out at Hudson Mountain, says, "Aww, Russ," or one of Granddaddy's old rallying cries: "Russell, you're the *shits*!"

It's just a phase, though, and we all know it. Russell will take a drink, look up at the night sky through the crazy sprawl of limbs above us, and he'll sigh. He'll be anchored, then, with Granddaddy and Uncle Jimmy and my father, Charlie, holding him down. He will stop talking of pipe sales, will stop speaking of Houston-town, and no longer be the shits. He'll just be looking up at the stars. Then Randy will belch and say, "That's better, Russ."

It's all a cycle, and I have little interest in the short term. I think it's the shits, too, when Russ starts talking about a single year. I want to talk about sixty-four years. And so do my uncle and father.

* * *

What Uncle Jimmy, who has a fierce, almost weepy pride in this clan of boys and men, does when he's in his cups at one or two A.M. and the thrill of all of us being together again consumes him, is talk about our family.

There are several Fort Worth Basses in Texas, and my grandfather had nothing to do with any of the other Basses. Granddaddy ran a country gas station on the outskirts of Forth Worth, out toward the village of Crowley, for forty years. Aside from the annual deer hunt, he took one vacation a year, to go fishing in Colorado each summer with my grandmother, who taught school.

My father and uncle grew up poor—wash-clothes-in-the-bathtub poor, for a while. They married young, had children young (the web, the roots, beginning to spread), and then, after a long time, they were poor no longer.

My father and mother had a tough go of it, at the beginning, too—before my father learned how to plumb the earth, how to reach deep. They hung the clothes out to dry in the West Texas wind.

My uncle, who has been spending too much time in Japan negotiating pipe deals, tells how the interpreters continue to ask him if he's one of those famous Fort Worth Basses. They're not talking about us, when they ask that.

My father, a geologist as well as a geophysicist, says he's been asked that question all over Texas, Louisiana, Mississippi, Alabama. Wherever he goes to find the oil and gas fields he's so good at discovering, they ask him.

He just says, "No." Perhaps he thinks about how it might have been if we were the wealthy Fort Worth Basses, instead of the other Fort Worth Basses, but I doubt it.

Pride can be a rough thing. It's not something easily eroded, nor is it easily buried.

My father and uncle are asked this question wherever they go. And I'm sure that along with their reply is the memory of a dusty, lonely gas station on the outskirts of town. They say, "No, I'm not of 'the Fort Worth Basses,' " and then they recall sitting in the station drinking a pop, playing, while their father—Granddaddy—sits behind the counter, waiting for business.

We were raised outdoors, and it's been the blessing of our life. My father didn't have to raise me outdoors. He didn't have to work to be a hunter and a fisherman in a rough, unpolished way. He had worked hard enough and succeeded well enough to raise me and my brothers any way he wanted. He chose the outdoors just as Granddaddy chose this rough cedar country.

Our legacy, our blessing, has been to grow up on the land and to take from it while giving back to it, too. It is right to try to emulate it: to learn from it, to have some spots of gentleness and gracefulness. We learned to give the land our memories and love, to give it back respect, to give it back everything—including, in time, our bodies.

At the campfire last year, Uncle Jimmy talked to us about what it means to be a Bass. He went from son to son, nephew to nephew, and brother to brother, clasping his big hand on each of our shoulders—chewing his big cigar—as he talked to us not about the things a Bass does or doesn't do, but about the manner in which they're done. It has to do with being on the outside of the world rather than wrapped up in the center and noise of it.

Granddaddy's asleep in his bed, by this time of night. But he's not far away; he's just inside the lodge. In his sleep, I like to think that he hears us: that some younger part of him hears what we're saying.

The stars flash and glimmer, above us; the wind carries the smell of cedar to us. It's a cool night in the fall, and the fire is warm. The wind creaks the rafters of the big lodge behind us, the one we built by hand over the course of one summer. Our lives seem to have everything to do with rocks, with the earth: with things that last. Cool night air slides down off the top of the Burned-Off Hill and washes our faces. It's late. In the morning we'll go out into the woods again and move across the land.

My father taught me the boundaries and borders, the secrets of the Deer Pasture, and taught me how to hunt just as Granddaddy had taught him. Even now, as I write this, I'm not remembering those old pictures of deer-gone-by, deer on the hoods of old jeeps, photos of past hunts before I was even born, but rather the sound my boots make when I'm climbing one of those sandstone ridges over on the back side and when I dislodge a pebble that rolls down into the canyon. I'm remembering the red-rock canyons and the first time my father hiked with me back to Buck Hill and showed me the view.

This is one of the ways to write about my father: to write about the land he has chosen to keep walking across, and our place on it as a whole—the *net* of us, my family's men. If I had a choice—if I had to make one—I'd rather be in the woods than have money. I'd rather be happy than famous: if that were some kind of choice that needed making. A long time ago, the men in my family decided to turn to the woods, rather than to the city; to spend more and more time in the woods, as much time as they could.

The view from the tops of these ridges at the Deer Pasture lets you see damn near everything. How far? Since it is the nature of a family of geologists to measure things in terms of years rather than miles, that horizon off to the east—where the flat top of Hudson Mountain looms—is sixty-four years distant . . . and changing every year, moving away from us all the time, even though we chase it.

I have to believe that we are gaining on it. It seems that we are.

197

ABOUT THE CONTRIBUTORS

Charles Gaines, novelist, screenwriter, and author of several nonfiction books, lives in New Hampshire and Nova Scotia. His books include *Pumping Iron*, *Stay Hungry*, and *Dangler*. He is currently working on a series of nonfiction books with the actor Arnold Schwarzenegger.

Kent Nelson is the author of three novels, the most recent being *Language in the Blood*, and two collections of short stories. His fiction has received many awards, including a Pushcart Prize and O'Henry selection for *The Best American Short Stories*. He lives in New Hampshire.

Stratis Haviaras is the author of five collections of poetry and two novels. *The Heroic Age*, a novel, is his most recent book. He is curator of the Poetry and Farnsworth rooms at Harvard University and coeditor of the *Harvard Book Review*. He lives in Cambridge, Massachusetts.

John Cole is the author of ten books—his latest is *Tarpon Quest*, published by Lyons & Burford—and scores of articles for national magazines. He lives and works in Key West.

Laton McCartney grew up on cattle ranches in Colorado and Wyoming before moving to Manhattan, where he works as a magazine editor and writer. He is the author of *Friends in High Places: The Bechtel Story*, published by Simon and Schuster. He is currently working on a book about the settlement of the American West called *South Pass* for Doubleday.

Donald Hall lives in New Hampshire, where he works as a free-lance writer. Some of his essays are collected in *Fathers Playing Catch with Sons*, *Seasons at Eagle Pond*, and *Here at Eagle Pond*. His books of poetry include *The One Day* and *Old and New Poems*.

Nick Lyons, a former professor of English at Hunter College, is now president of Lyons & Burford, Publishers. He has published nine books, and several hundred of his essays have appeared in the *New York Times*, *Harper's*, *The Yale Review*, *Fly Fisherman*, *Field & Stream*, and elsewhere. He lives in New York City.

Wesley McNair is a recipient of a Guggenheim Fellowship and two NEA fellowships. He is the author of four volumes of verse: *The Faces of Americans in 1853*, which won the Devins Award; *The Town of No*; *My Brother Running*; and the forthcoming *Twelve Journeys in Maine*. He lives and works in Maine.

David Ewing Duncan is a free-lance writer who contributes to *Smithsonian* and the *Atlantic*. He is the author of *From Cape to Cairo*, and is currently at work on a biography of the explorer Hernando de Soto. He lives in Maryland.

Kenneth Barrett lives in Bozeman, Montana, where he works as development director for a nonprofit environmental organization. He is currently working on a collection of essays about hunting.

William Kittredge teaches at the University of Montana. His most recent book is *A Hole in the Sky*, a memoir, published by Alfred A. Knopf.

Jeff Hull is a free-lance writer who lives in Montana. His fiction and nonfiction have appeared in many periodicals, including the *Southern Review* and *Yacht*. He is currently working on his first novel.

David Seybold's short stories and essays have appeared in numerous magazines and anthologies. *Fathers and Sons* is the fifth anthology he has edited. He is currently completing his first collection of essays, called *A Fine Excess*.

Dan Gerber is a poet, short story writer, and novelist. His most recent books include *Grass Fires*, *A Voice from the River*, and *A Last Bridge Home: New and Selected Poems*. He lives by a small lake in rural western Michigan.

Joseph McElroy's most recent novels are *Women and Men* and *The Letter Left to Me*. Forthcoming is a book of novellas and short stories, and the first two novels in a sequence. He lives in New York and New Mexico.

Verlyn Klinkenborg is a Briggs-Copeland assistant professor at Harvard University; his latest book is *The Last Fine Time*, published by Alfred A. Knopf. His essays have appeared in many magazines, including *The New Yorker*, *Esquire*, and *Harper's*. He lives in Massachusetts.

Russell Chatham is an author, publisher, and painter who lives in Montana. His books include *Angler's Coast*, *The Missouri Headwaters*, and, most recently, *Dark Waters*.

Sydney Lea is the author of five collections of poetry, the most recent being *The Blainville Testament* and *Prayer for the Little City*. His novel *A Place in Mind* was published in 1989. He is presently at work on a collection of naturalist essays called *Hunting Up the Seton Ram*. He lives in New Hampshire.

Jim Fergus is a free-lance writer who lives in Colorado. His work has appeared in such periodicals as *Outside Magazine*, the *Paris Review*, and *Harrowsmith's Country Life*. He is the author of the book *A Hunter's Road*, which was recently published by Henry Holt.

Robert F. Jones's novel *Blood Tide* was named one of the best thrillers of the year by the *New York Times* in 1990. His most recent book, *The Fishing Doctor*, appeared this spring. Two other works of nonfiction will be published later this year. He lives in Vermont.

Robert Olmstead lives in Pennsylvania, where he is writer-in-residence at Dickinson College. His fiction has appeared in *Black Warrior Review*, *Granta*, and several other literary reviews and journals. His previous books are *River Dogs*, a collection of stories, and the novels *Soft Water* and *Trail of Heart's Blood Wherever We Go*.

William Hjortsberg has published six works of fiction, including *Alp* and *Gray Matters*. His novel *Falling Angel* has been translated into fourteen languages. Among his screen credits are *Legend* and *Angel Heart*. He lives in Montana.

Rick Bass lives in Montana, where he writes collections of short stories and essays. His books include *The Watch*, *Oil Notes*, and *Winter*. He is currently working on a book about wolves for Clark City Press.

ABOUT THE EDITOR

David Seybold's previous anthologies are *Waters Swift and Still* (with Craig Woods), *Seasons of the Hunter* (with Robert Elman), *Seasons of the Angler*, and *Boats*. He lives in New Hampshire.